ANDROID SMARTPHONES FOR SENIORS MADE EASY

Connecting with Friends & Family

By James Bernstein

Bernstein, James
Android Smartphones for Seniors Made Easy
Part of the Computers For Seniors Made Easy series

For more information on reproducing sections of this book or sales of
this book, go to **www.madeeasybookseries.com**

Contents

Introduction

Smartphones have been around for many years now, and most people are so used to having one that they are just as much a way of life as having a TV or refrigerator in your house. And the younger generation doesn't even know of a life without smartphones, and, between you and me, probably can't function without one!

For those of us that have been around longer than smartphones, you may find it's not as easy getting as comfortable with using one compared to a teenager. Many people today still don't even like to use their home computer and taking on another electronic device can be too much for them. And, worst of all, these smartphones usually don't come with instruction manuals, so you are forced to learn how to use them on your own or with the help of others.

The goal of this book is to get you started on your smartphone adventure without confusing and irritating you at the same time. I find that if you explain things like someone is a total beginner, even if they are not, it makes that topic much easier to understand, and that is the way this book was written, so that anyone can make sense of the content without feeling lost.

This book will cover a wide variety of topics such as initial phone setup and configuration, installing and using apps, texting, making phone calls, using the camera, browsing the internet, getting driving directions with the navigation feature and so on. One thing I will stress over and over throughout this book is that not all Android-based smartphones are alike. There are many upon many manufacturers of smartphones that use the Android operating system (hence the name), and many of them like to use their own interface to customize the way the phone looks and feels to make it unique. For example, a Samsung Android phone will not look and operate exactly the same as an LG Android phone.

For the most part, all Android smartphones do most of the same things, but how you do them is where you will see the differences. So, if you find something in this book that doesn't match exactly with your specific phone, then that is most likely the reason, and you may have to do a little poking around to get the results you are looking for. I will be using a Google Pixel smartphone for my examples in this book, and I like the Google phones because they tend to keep the look and feel of the pure Android interface without adding any fancy "skins" to the phone (which can make things more complicated, in my opinion). This is where iPhone users have the advantage since an iPhone is an iPhone and only Apple makes them and doesn't let anyone else make their own version.

So on that note, break out your phone and your reading glasses if you need them, and let's get down to business!

Chapter 1 – Smartphone Basics

Since you are reading this book, it's safe to say that you are the proud owner of an Android based smartphone. Keep in mind that Android is not the brand of your phone but rather the operating system or software that runs your phone. It's just like if you have a computer that uses Microsoft Windows with Windows being the operating system and the brand is something like Dell or HP etc.

There are many manufacturers of smartphones including Google, Samsung, LG, Motorola, HTC and many more. And speaking of Google, they are the ones who created the Android operating system and license it to other phone manufacturers to use on their smartphones.

Smartphones vs. Regular Cell Phones

If this is your first smartphone, there is a good chance that you have upgraded from a regular cell phone and have most likely noticed that it's quite different from your old phone! Smartphones are pretty much handheld computers that can make phone calls and are actually much more powerful than the computers we used not too long ago.

The main difference between a smartphone and a regular cellphone is that you can go online and use the internet as well as use the phone as a GPS to help you navigate to any destination you need to get to. Of course you can also install apps such as games on your smartphone, but many regular phones have this ability as well. But the apps you can use on your smartphone are far more advanced than anything you can use on a regular phone.

Smartphones will also have a touchscreen meaning you can use your finger to manipulate items on the screen the same way you use a mouse on your computer. You can even do things like hold your finger down on certain items to drag them around or bring up additional options. But for the most part you will use your finger to "tap" on items compared to clicking on items using your mouse on your computer. If you have ever used a tablet\iPad, your phone will work in a similar manner in regard to how you manipulate the screen.

Some regular cellphones will have keyboards on them which makes texting and other tasks easier while smartphones will have an on screen touch keyboard as seen in figure 1.1.

Figure 1.1

Another thing you will notice from figure 1.1 is the difference in screen size between the two types of phones. Different smartphone models will have various size screens ranging from 3 to 6+ inches. The average screen size will be between 5 and 6 inches for most models. The screen resolution and image quality will be much higher on a smartphone as well.

Overall, a smartphone is much more powerful than a regular cellphone and has so many more features that there is really no comparison between the two. Many people who resist the pressure to switch to a smartphone are usually glad they did once they see how much they can do with one. You might be the type who says, "I only use my phone to make calls," but that will quickly change once you get your new smartphone!

Plans and Payment
Buying a smartphone and choosing a plan can be as painful as buying a new car if you don't know what you are looking for and what the available options mean. You will have to decide on things such as how much data you think you will use per month, if you want to buy the phone outright or make payments on it, and whether or not you need unlimited text messages.

The most difficult decision you will need to make is how much data you will be using per month. Smartphones have data plans that only allow you to do things online such as browse the web, stream music, or watch videos, which consumes data as you go. If you use more data than allowed, then you will be charged extra for going over, and that can add up quickly. And, if you get more data than you need, you will be paying for it whether you use it or not.

Some plans allow you to transfer any unused data over to your balance for the next month, giving you a little cushion in case you have a heavy data usage month. Fortunately, you should be able to change your data plan at any time to give you more data or take away data that you don't need to use or pay for, so it might take a little trial and error on your part to see what works best for you. You might want to start with a mid-range data plan and then adjust it from there. There are also unlimited plans where you can use as much data as you want but the monthly charge will be more for this type of plan.

When you are connected to your wireless (Wi-Fi) at home or at another location, you do not use your plan data so anything you do while connected to a wireless connection will technically be free. Plus doing things such as making calls and texting doesn't count against your data plan.

As for calling and texting, most plans these days will give you unlimited calling and texting, so you don't need to worry about using too many minutes or sending too many text messages.

If you don't get the free phone that comes with many plans, then you will need to either buy the phone outright or make payments on it. If you choose to make payments on it, then you usually get stuck in a two year contract paying it off. Even if you buy the phone outright, make sure you don't get put in a contract that you don't want to be in unless it benefits you to be in that contract. By the way, the free phones are free for a reason, and if this is going to be your first smartphone experience, then it might get ruined by one of these cheap phones!

Android vs. iPhone
There is most likely some reason you chose to get an Android-based smartphone over an Apple iPhone. It might have been because there was a special deal that included the phone, or a friend or relative convinced you that you would be better off with an Android, etc. Whatever the reason, it appears that you have made the right choice!

As I mentioned earlier in the book, an iPhone is an iPhone while there are many manufacturers of Android smartphones, and they will differ to some degree as to how they look and how they function. If you are Internet savvy, then you can usually find the answer you are looking for online, and once you get better at using your phone and figuring out how to do things, you can eventually figure out how to do almost anything you need to do without wanting to throw your phone out the window!

I always describe iPhones as smartphones for people who just want to be told what to do and how to do it, while Android smartphones are for those who like to have control over their phones and tweak them to work the way they want them to. But at the same time, iPhones tend to be a little more secure since they are locked down by Apple and they don't let anyone tweak anything that shouldn't be allowed to do so. iPhones also tend to be more expensive and are one of the best quality phones you can get when it comes to how they are built. There are many great quality Android phones as well. Apple does a good job at making the operating system for their iPhone work similarly to their iPad tablets, as well as their desktop computers and laptops.

Figure 1.2 shows an example of a typical iPhone, while figure 1.3 shows a Google Pixel. Overall, most Android smartphones look very similar, and you might even think the iPhone looks similar to them as well (which in fact, it does a little).

Figure 1.2

Figure 1.3

Since not all Android phones are the same, yours might look different from figure 1.3 and also might vary a bit from the screenshots I will be using throughout this book. This is one of the main problems when it comes to teaching Android owners how to use their phones.

Chapter 2 – Setting Up Your New Phone

When you get your new smartphone, you will have a couple of options when it comes to setting it up for its initial power on and configuration. You can have the store you bought it from do it for you (most likely for a fee), or you can try and tackle it yourself. If you buy it online, then you will be stuck setting it up yourself unless you take it to your local cell provider store and have them set it up for you. If you are feeling a little techy, I would suggest that you do the setup yourself because it will help you get used to how the phone works, and then you will know firsthand how it has been configured.

Initial Configuration

The first time you power on your new smartphone you will be asked a few questions to help configure your phone for its initial usage. These questions will vary depending on what phone you have, and what version of the Android operating system you are running. Just like with the phones themselves, Google updates its operating system from time to time to add improvements and security features.

Even though your phone should come with the battery at least somewhat charged, you might want to connect it to the wall to charge it for a little bit before starting your phone. Smartphones will come with a wall charger and a detachable USB cable that can be used to connect to your computer for charging, as well as transferring pictures and other files. If you take a look at figure 2.1, you will see that you can use the USB cable to connect to the wall charger, or you can connect the USB end to your computer to charge it that way.

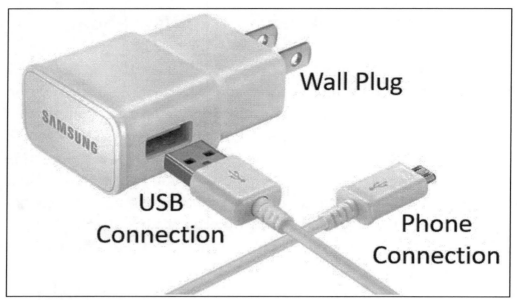

Figure 2.1

To power on your new smartphone, hold down the power button on the side until you see something appear on the screen, and then let go. It will take a minute to start up to the point where you will need to start inputting information. Your phone will most likely have one button for power and then two others for volume up and down, and their location will vary depending on your phone model.

Once the phone boots up, you will begin the setup process and be prompted to answer several questions. Here are some possible configuration questions you might have to answer since, once again, this process will vary:

- Selecting your language.
- Activating your phone on your provider's network (this should be an automatic process).
- Connecting your phone to your home wireless (Wi-Fi) network (be sure to have your wireless password on hand if you don't already know it).
- Configuring the fingerprint scanner if you have one (optional).
- Allowing your phone to download any updates.

- Signing into or creating a Google account to be used with your phone.
- Configuring email accounts.
- Setting up security options

For the most part, these configuration settings should be fairly easy to set up so try and have the information from the list above ready for when you activate your phone. You can usually skip some of the steps such as the wireless setup or configuring email accounts if you don't have the information handy and then take care of it later after your phone is up and running.

If you get stuck on something, you can usually call the store you bought the phone from or contact your service provider for assistance. Just be ready to stay on hold for a while!

Logging in With Your Google Account
There are a few reasons why Google wants you to have a Google account associated with your phone, but the main reason is to keep track of what apps you download from the Play Store, which is the place you search for apps to install on your phone. There are many free apps, and many that cost money, so having a Google account makes it easy to keep track of what apps you have and which apps you have paid for. You don't need to set up any payment information for apps if you don't want to but will only be able to download free apps this way, which is usually fine for most people (including myself).

Another benefit to having a Google account is that it stores not only your app information but also your contacts, so that way if you get a new phone, all you need to do is log in with your Google account and all of your contacts will be imported and you are ready to go. You can also go to *Google Contacts* on your computer and access your contacts from there just by signing in.

Signing up for a Google account also gives you a Gmail account just for doing so. Gmail is Google's email service, and it's free to use and very popular. It's also easy to check your Gmail messages from anywhere you have Internet access. Keep in mind that you don't need to use Gmail once you sign up, but it will be there in case you change your mind.

If you already have a Gmail account, then that means you have a Google account, and all you need to do is enter your Gmail address and password during setup and you will be ready to go, and all your Google contacts and email will be imported into your new phone. You don't have to use your existing Google account and can create a new one during the setup if you choose to do so. It is also possible to have multiple Gmail accounts on one phone if that's something you wish to do.

When you get to the Google account part of the setup, you will need to either type in your existing Google\Gmail email address and its associated password, or you will need to create a new Google account. You will be able to create a new account on the spot, but you will need to think of a username for your account that is not already taken.

If you type in a name that is already in use by someone else, you will be notified and informed that you need to try another name. You might even be given some suggestions that are not in use. For example, if you tried to use **jsmith@gmail.com** and it's in use, then your phone might suggest something like **jsmith1287** and you can either take their suggestion or try something else. You will then need to come up with a password for your account. You should always make it somewhat complex with upper and lower case letters and maybe a number and special character such as **!,@,#,$, or %,** etc.

Connecting to Your Wi-Fi (Wireless Internet)

I mentioned before that you will be prompted to configure your wireless Internet connection during the setup of your phone, but if you are not at home when you set up your phone, you will not be able to do this and will have to skip this step. Or, if for some reason something changes with your wireless connection, this will apply to reconfiguring Wi-Fi to work with your phone.

To configure your wireless connection, you will need to find your phone's settings icon, which usually looks like an image of a gear. You might have this on your main screen (called the home screen), and if not, you will find it with your other apps, most likely in alphabetical order.

Another way to get to your settings is to swipe down from the notification area (discussed later) at the top of the phone and then look for the settings gear icon. Once you are at your settings, look for something that says *Network & internet* (yours might be named slightly different).

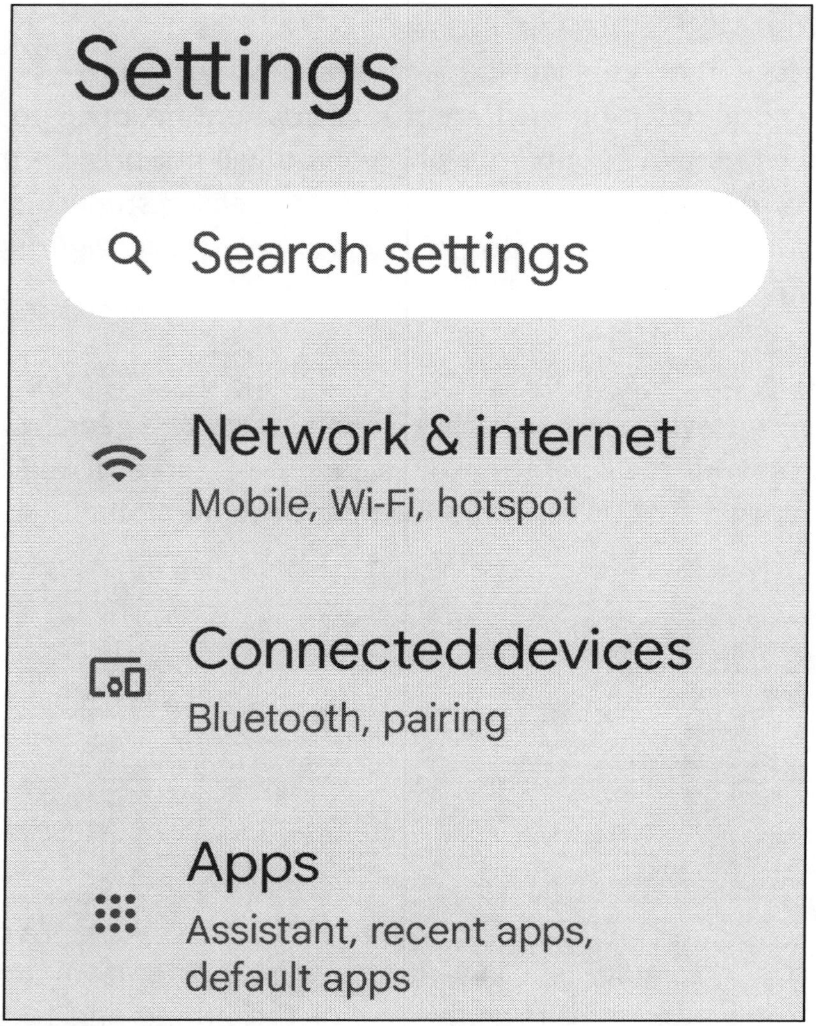

Settings

🔍 Search settings

📶 **Network & internet**
Mobile, Wi-Fi, hotspot

🖥️ **Connected devices**
Bluetooth, pairing

⠿ **Apps**
Assistant, recent apps,
default apps

Figure 2.2

Once you are there you will look for the wireless name that matches the one you have configured at home (or wherever else you are trying to connect). Also be sure that Wi-Fi is enabled otherwise you will not be able to access any wireless connection.

Figure 2.3 shows some of the wireless access points in the range of my phone. You will most likely see other access point names when connecting to your wireless unless you are in an area with no neighbors close by.

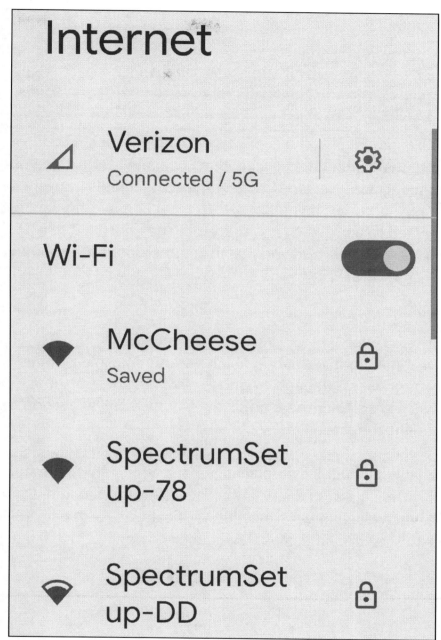

Internet

Verizon
Connected / 5G

Wi-Fi

McCheese
Saved

SpectrumSet
up-78

SpectrumSet
up-DD

Figure 2.3

The padlock icon next to the name indicates that it's a secured connection and you will need to know the password to connect to it.

 Just because a wireless internet connection doesn't have a password doesn't mean you should necessarily connect to it. If you do not know where this connection is originating from and you connect to it, it could end up giving someone access to your phone.

Once you find the connection name that is associated with your wireless internet access, you would then tap on the name to enter the password for your account. If you enter the correct password, you will then be connected to your Wi-Fi and therefore the internet itself. This password will be the same one you use for your computer at home if you are connected wirelessly to the internet.

Screen Brightness Level

One thing that I have noticed when using various Android phones is that the screen tends not to be as bright as I like it to be. Fortunately, your phone will have a brightness adjustment which will allow you to control how bright the screen is.

There are usually a couple of places where you can make this adjustment. Figure 2.4 shows the brightness adjustment bar at the top of the screen when I pull down from the notification area. I can then use my finger to slice the brightness level up or down.

Figure 2.4

Figures 2.5 and 2.6 show how to get to the brightness settings from the main settings area that we used for the wireless setup. You would first go to the settings and look for a section called *Display* or something similar.

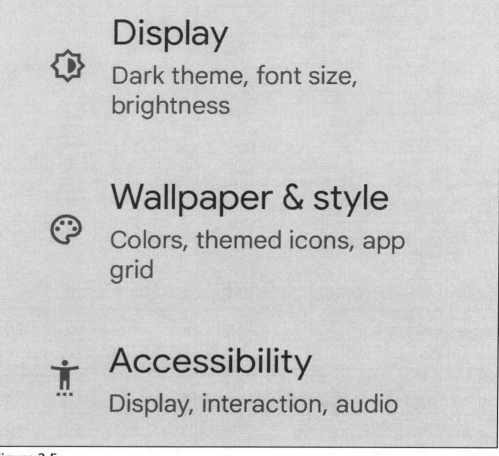

Figure 2.5

Then you can tap on the brightness level and set it to a level that works for your eyes. The section called adaptive brightness is used to automatically adjust the brightness level based on how bright it is outside or in the room. I find that this usually doesn't make the screen bright enough, so I turn it off and manually adjust the brightness level. This option might be named something different on your phone so keep that in mind.

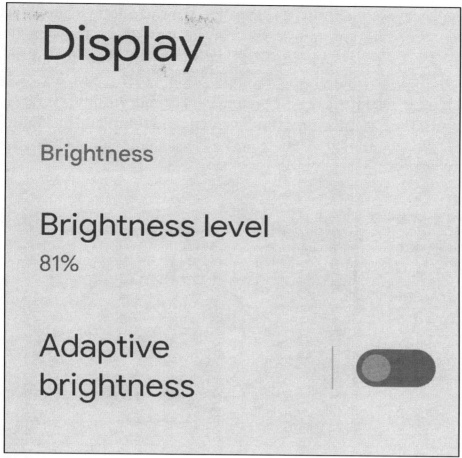

Figure 2.6

Screen Protectors and Cases

You might have noticed that your new smartphone feels a little on the delicate side, and maybe even a little slippery when you are holding it. These phone manufacturers focus so much on making their products look sleek that they tend to not think so much about making them durable.

When it comes to protecting your phone, you should defiantly get a case for it to help keep it safe from scratches, from dropping it, or even setting it down on a rough surface. There are many types of cases to choose from, ranging from super slim to super rugged. I don't recommend getting one from the store you got the phone from unless you like to over-pay for things. You can go online somewhere like Amazon and get a great case for $10. Just make sure you are getting one for your exact phone. For example, don't just get a Samsung Galaxy case and assume it will fit on any version but rather search for a Samsung Galaxy 21 case or whatever your model might be. Figure 2.7 shows a few examples of the types of cases you can get for your phone.

Figure 2.7

Another protective item you might want to look into is getting a screen protector, which will protect your screen from scratches and potential cracks. There are two main kinds you can get for your phone. The first is a plastic film that sticks on the glass and offers protection mainly for scratches. The next type of screen protector is made out of tempered glass and offers more protection when it comes to cracking your screen if you drop your phone. The idea is that the screen protector itself will crack rather than your actual screen. When this happens, all you need to do is take it off and put on a new one. Once again, you can get these online much cheaper than you can at the phone store, and once again make sure you get one that is made for your specific phone, otherwise it won't fit.

Figure 2.8

Chapter 3 – Using Your Phone

Now that you have your new phone setup (hopefully), it's time to start using the phone for what it was meant to be used for, pretty much everything! Well maybe not everything, but you just may find yourself using it way more than you ever thought you would.

Today's smartphones are capable of doing much more than most people will ever do with them. Some people prefer to use their phones for school and work rather than using a computer for these kinds of tasks. Personally, I think having a large screen, keyboard and mouse is much easier to use but I suppose if you were raised with smartphones, they tend to become a part of you.

Home Screen and Apps List
Once you get your phone up and running, you will most likely spend most of your time on the home screen since that will be where you will have your most commonly used app icons located. You can think of your home screen as being similar to your desktop on your computer where you go to open all of your programs.

When you install a new app, it will usually place an icon on your home screen unless it's full. If that's the case, it will place the icon on one of your other screens. You can get to these other screens by swiping left. The number of additional screens you will have will vary depending on your phone model.

Figure 3.1 shows the home screen and second screen of a typical Android phone. The main home screen is on the left, and at the bottom you will find what is called the app tray or app drawer which is highlighted with a box around it. This is where you will find your most commonly used apps such as your phone, text, contacts, camera, web browser etc.

Figure 3.1

You will also notice that there is a search box at the bottom of the screen that can be used to search the internet. Your search box might be located at the top or middle of the screen and many times it can be moved to a different location or even removed to make room for more app icons.

Depending on your phone's configuration and model, you may also have a home and back button at the bottom of the screen. The home button can be used to take you back to your home screen and the back button can be used to go back to the previous screen while in an app.

Many Android phones are configured where you need to swipe from the right side of the screen over to the left to go back but often times you can change this option so you have the back and home buttons displayed.

The screen on the right side of figure 3.1 is the secondary screen and looks very similar to the home screen. This is where you can store app icons that you don't use as much. You can also long hold on an icon to drag it to a different location. By long hold I mean holding your finger down on the icon rather than just tapping once on it. For most phones, you can also hold and drag the icon to the top of the screen to have an option to remove it or uninstall the app as seen in figure 3.2. Removing the icon will not uninstall the app but simply just take the icon off of your home screen or one of your other screens.

Not all of your apps will be listed on the home screen or your secondary home screens so if you can't find something, you will need to check your main app screen. This can usually be accessed by swiping up from the bottom of your phone and then you can scroll through every app that is installed on your phone and open them as needed. You can even long hold on an app icon and drag it to one of your home screens if you want an easier way to access it.

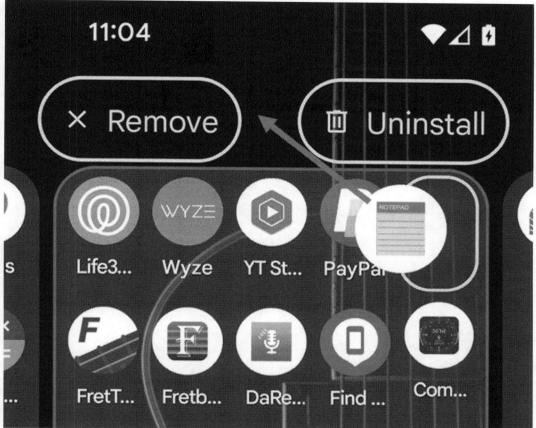

Figure 3.2

 Your smartphone will most likely come with a lot of preinstalled applications of which many you will most likely never use. If you want to keep your screens tidier, you can always remove the app icon or even uninstall an app if you think you will never use it. Just be aware that some apps are not able to be uninstalled.

Changing Your Background Image

One thing you will most likely notice when you first get your phone is that it will come with some type of background wallpaper image that may or may not really like. Fortunately, it's easy to change this picture to some other one that will be included with your phone or even a picture that you have taken yourself.

The process for changing your background picture will vary between phone models but what you should be able to do most of the time is long hold on a blank area of your home screen and see if you get an option that says something like change wallpaper or something similar as seen in figure 3.3.

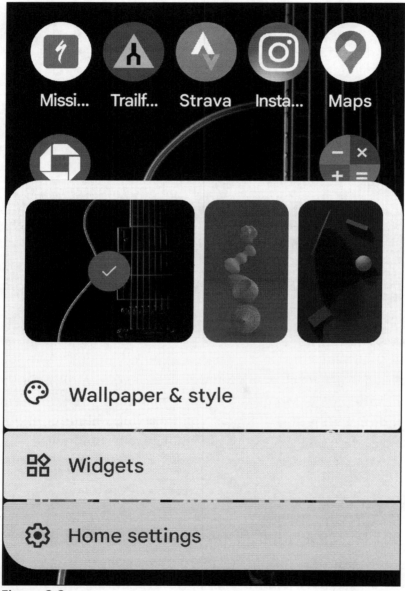

Figure 3.3

When you go to your wallpaper settings, you will be able to choose from existing photos on your phone that you have taken, or you can choose a photo from one of the many categories that come with the phone.

Figure 3.4

After you choose a photo, you will most likely be asked if you want to apply it to the home screen, lock screen or both. The lock screen is what you see when your phone is locked when you press the screen on button (power button).

Figure 3.5

On a quick side note, I want to go over the buttons on your phone in case you don't know what they do. Most Android smartphones will have three buttons, and usually they are on the right side of the phone but of course this can vary between models.

Figure 3.6 shows that you have the top button which is usually the one for turning the screen on and off. It can also be used to silence a phone call yet still let it ring. Then you will have up and down volume buttons that are really close together and can even be one button that can be pressed from the top or bottom as needed.

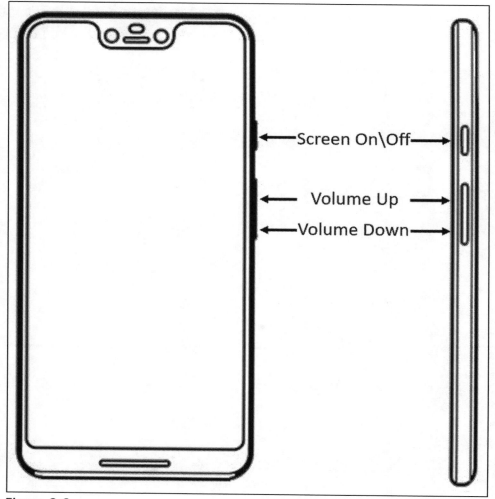

Screen On\Off

Volume Up

Volume Down

Figure 3.6

Notification Area

As you receive phone calls, voicemails, emails and so on, you will receive notifications in what is called the notification area at the very top of the phone. These are meant to make it easy for you to see when something important comes to your phone and is also an easy way to see if you have missed something while away from your phone.

Not every type of event will give you a notification and you can actually choose which types of events will show notifications and which will not so keep that in mind if you are ever feeling extra techy!

Figure 3.6 shows the notification area with a box around it. Within that notification area it shows a missed call, new voicemail and new email.

Figure 3.7

If I pull down from the top of the screen where the notification icons are located, I will see the three different notifications that I had at the top in more detail. I can then tap on one to open it or swipe them to the right to dismiss them.

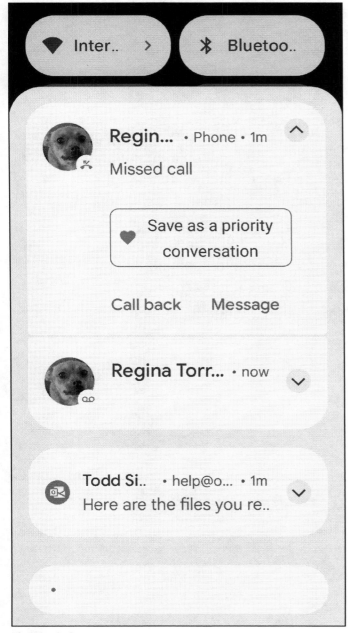

Figure 3.8

Some phones will even show you your notifications on your lock screen so all you need to do is press the screen on button to see them as shown in figure 3.9.

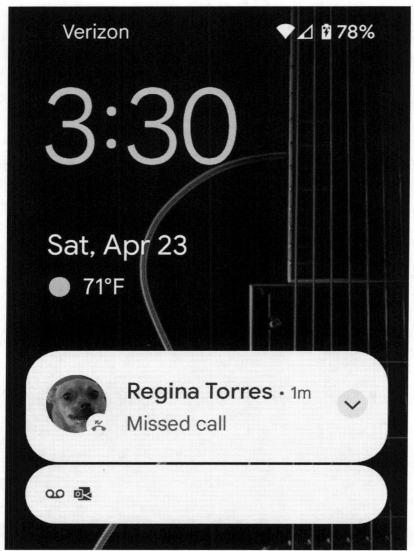

Figure 3.9

You will most likely find yourself using the notification quite a bit, especially if you tend to get a lot of emails, phone calls and text messages.

Adding Contact Information

To make it easier to send text messages and make phone calls, you should add people who you contact on a regular basis to your contact list. This way you do not need to remember their phone number in order to call or text them. These contacts can also be used for email depending on what email service an app you use (AOL, Gmail, Yahoo etc.).

To view your contacts, look for the Contacts icon which will be a blue circle with a white silhouette figure inside of it.

If you configured a new Google account, you will not have any contacts shown. But if you added your existing Google\Gmail account to your phone then you should see all the contacts that you have created or saved in your Google account listed in alphabetical order. You should also have a search box where you can search by name, phone number, email address etc.

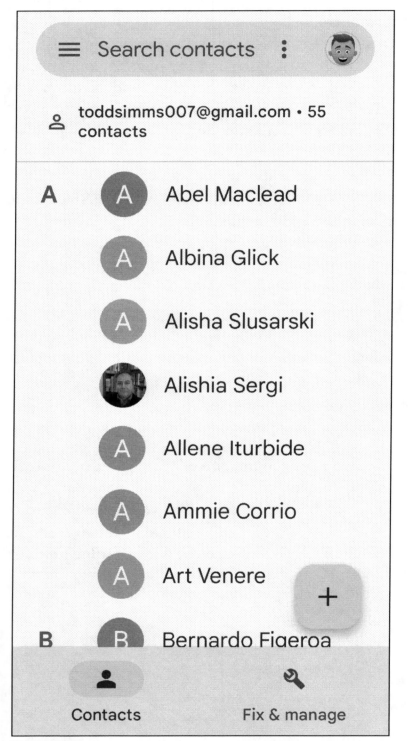

Figure 3.10

To add a new contact, tap on the + button and then fill in any information you wish to save for this new contact. You can also add a photo from your phone to go along with your contact.

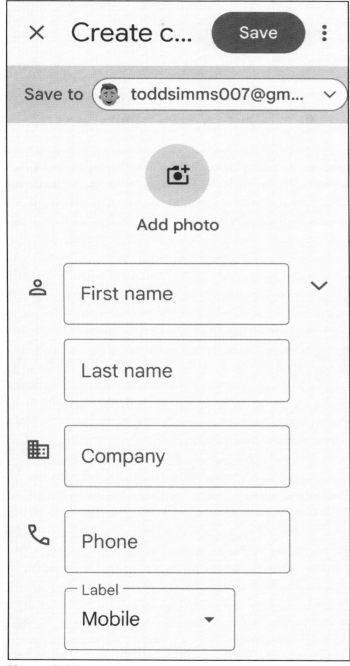

Figure 3.11

When you are finished, simply tap on Save and your new contact will be added to your phone. I will be showing you how to use your contacts for phone calls and texting later in the book.

Making and Receiving Phone Calls

I would say that one of the main reasons for getting a smartphone is to make phone calls but if you are of the younger generation, this is most likely not the case! But for those of us who still like to actually talk to people, we can use our phones to call them quite easily.

If you had a regular cellphone in the past, then making calls shouldn't be too difficult to figure out. All you need to do is tap on the phone icon to open your phone dialer (keypad).

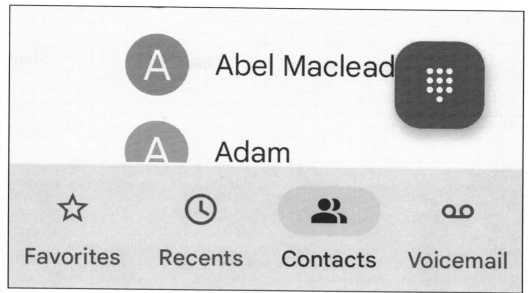

Figure 3.12

The phone app is used for more than making just phone calls. You can also use it to check your voicemail, see a listing of your recently made and received calls and view your contacts. You might have to tap on the number pad icon as seen at the top right of figure 3.12 to bring up the phone dialer so you can make a call.

Once you bring up the phone dialer, you might be shown a list of suggested contacts based on how often you call or receive calls from them. If you want to call one of these suggested contacts, you can simply tap on their name to start the call. Otherwise, you will need to dial the phone number itself and then tap the *Call* button to initiate the call.

Figure 3.13

Many phone service providers require you to dial the area code before making a call, even if the number you are calling is in the same area code as you are. So if you get a message saying the number cannot be completed as dialed, this might be the reason.

Once you have a call in progress, you will then have a red hang up button that you can press to end the call. If the person on the other end hangs up first, then you do not need to do anything.

When someone calls you, your phone will ring using its default ringtone, which you may or may not like. I will be discussing how to change your ringtone later in the chapter. When you hear and see your phone ringing, you will have the option to answer the call by tapping on the green *Answer* button hanging up on the person using the red *Decline* button (figure 3.14). When you hang up on a person without answering, it will send them directly to your voicemail.

Your phone might have a *Screen* button which is used to screen your calls using the built in Google Assistant (discussed later) to ask who's calling and why. You will get a real-time transcript of how the caller responds. Then if you like their answer, you can choose a suggested response, pick up the call, or hang up. If you think this is a feature you might want to use, you can try it out with a friend in the same room to get a better idea of what the person on the other end will hear.

Figure 3.14 shows how the incoming call will look when your phone screen is locked. You will be able to answer, decline or screen the call from this screen.

Figure 3.14

Figure 3.15 shows how an incoming call will look when you are using your phone. To answer, you would swipe up on the green phone picture and to decline you would swipe down. Your phone might look a little different so keep that in mind. If you have a Reply button for an incoming call, you can use that to send them a text message on the spot rather than answer the call. It will have some standard choices such as "I will call you right back", or you can type in your own.

You will also notice that if you have the caller in your contact list, it will show their name on the call and also show the picture you added for them.

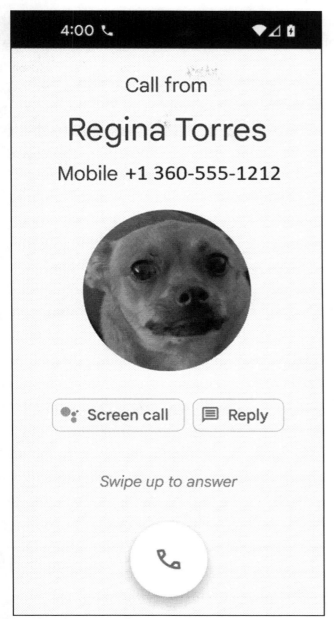

Figure 3.15

Calling Contacts & Adding Callers to Contacts

Once you have your friends and family's information stored in your contacts, it's much easier to call them since you don't need to type in their phone number or even remember it!

To call someone from your contacts, simply open your contacts and scroll down until you find their name. Then you will tap on their name and then tap on the Call icon, and it will instantly call their phone number. If you have more than one phone number stored for a person, you will be promoted to choose the number you want to call. You can also start typing their name in the search box and it will try and figure out who you want to call based on what you are typing as you go along.

Figure 3.16

Now let's say you received a call from someone that you don't have in your contacts, and you want to add that person to your contacts. Rather than start from scratch creating a new contact, you can go to your recent calls and find the number that called you. Then you can tap on the *Add contact* button to bring up the new contact screen where you can simply add the name related to that number and save it as a contact on your phone.

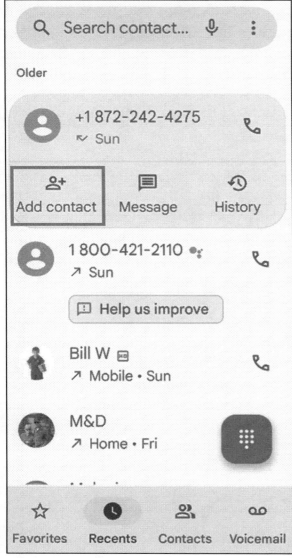

Figure 3.17

Reporting and Blocking Spam Calls

One common problem these days is the ever increasing amount of spam calls that we receive almost on a daily basis. Fortunately, we can report spam calls and block these numbers to try and decrease the number of calls that we get.

Once you know that a call you have received was spam, you can go into your call history and find the number that called you. Then you can long hold on the phone number and see if you have a block or report spam option as seen in figure 3.18. You may have this option shown somewhere else on your phone and may have to search for it.

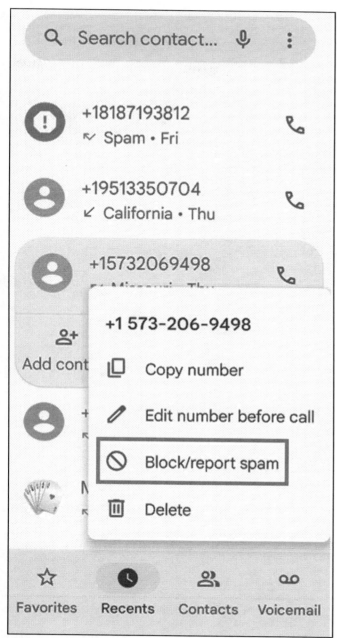

Figure 3.18

You may also have a box you can check to report the call as spam which should further help to prevent you from getting calls or text messages from that number.

Figure 3.19

After you block/report it, you should then see it in your call history marked as blocked. If you realize that the number is actually ok, you can come here and unblock it to allow calls from that number to come through next time as seen in figure 3.20.

 Many of these scammers have multiple phone numbers that they use to attempt to rip you off. So if you block one, you might find yourself getting the same call from a different number and will have to keep blocking numbers until the call stops.

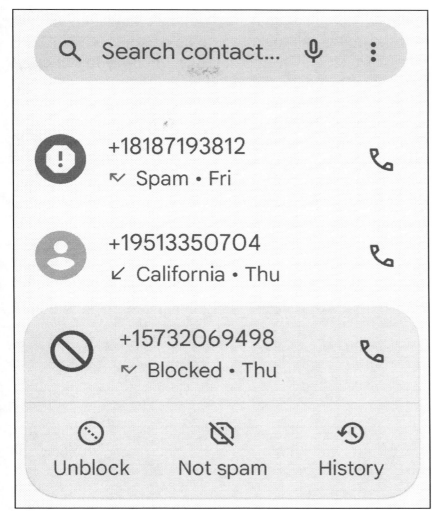

Figure 3.20

Checking Your Voicemail

If you are not around to answer your phone or do not feel like taking a call, it will be sent to your voicemail after a certain number of rings. Depending on your cell service provider, you might have to call into your voicemail using a number and then a passcode or PIN number and listen to them over the phone.

If you have the option to use what they call visual voicemail, you will be able to check your voicemail from an interface that looks sort of like what you would see for your email account. Many service providers offer visual voicemail for free and have other pay for types with additional features so if you don't have it on your phone, I recommend seeing if you can add it.

If you do have the service, you should be able to go to your phone app and find the voicemail section as seen in figure 3.21. Each of the listings here is a voicemail that you can play right from your phone without needing to dial into your voicemail account.

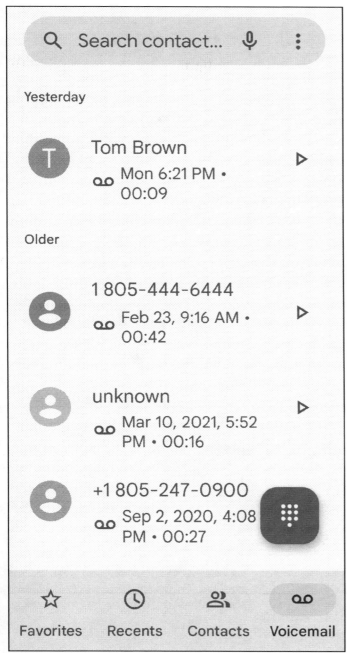

Figure 3.21

When you press the play button on one of these voicemails, you will
have the option to listen to the call and even play it over your speaker
phone by pressing the speaker icon. It will also show you the time of
the voicemail and how long it is (9 seconds in my example).

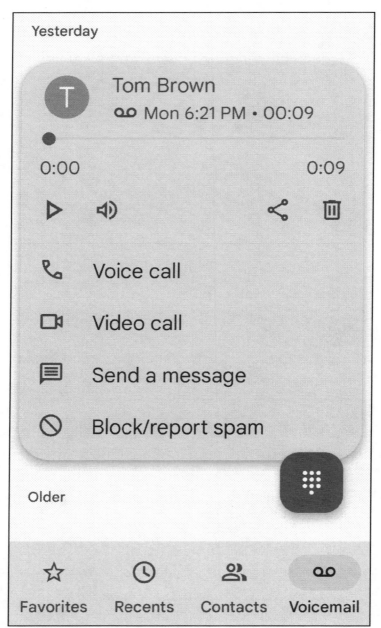

Figure 3.22

As you can see, you also have options to call the person back right from here as well as send a text message or even block the number. If you don't need to save the voicemail, you can delete it by tapping on the trash can icon.

Video Calls

Android phones have the ability to make video calls but how well this works will depend on who you are calling or who is calling you. If you are calling someone else who uses an Android smartphone, then it should work without any issues. But if you are trying to do a video call with an iPhone user then it most likely won't work without installing an additional app that is supported by both phones such as the popular **WhatsApp** app that many use to make calls to friends and family in other parts of the world.

Even though you can initiate a video call right from your main phone screen, the most trouble free way is to make a regular call first and then after you are connected, tap on the *Video call* icon as seen in figure 3.23.

Figure 3.23

Figure 3.24 shows how the video call invitation looks on the receiver's end. All they need to do is tap on *Answer* to start the video chat.

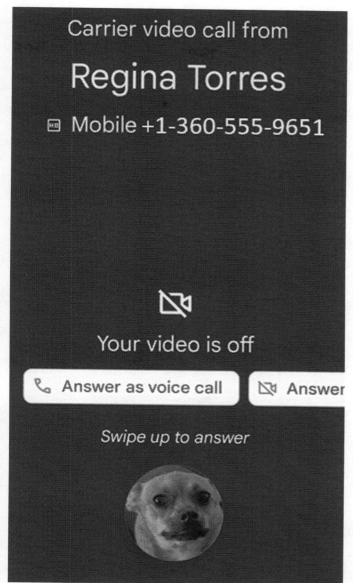

Figure 3.24

Figure 3.25 shows how a typical video call looks. You will be able to see the other person via their phone's camera so they need to be facing their phone towards themselves and be on speaker, otherwise you will be seeing the side of their head! You can also use the *Flip camera* button to switch to the camera on the other side of the phone if you want to show them something on your end for example.

Figure 3.25

If you want to end the call, simply tap on the red hang up button or you can also tap on *Camera off* to turn it back to a regular voice call.

Changing Your Ringtone

Your phone will come configured with a variety of built in sounds for various notifications such as a new email, voicemail or text message. It will also have a default ringtone for new calls and there is a good chance you will not like it and would prefer to use something else.

Fortunately, this is easy to change, and you should have many other ringtones to choose from.

While you are in your phone app, look for something that says settings, or you can also look for the three vertical dots icon (figure 3.26) which indicates that there are other options you will get when you tap on it. You will see these three vertical dots in many other apps as well.

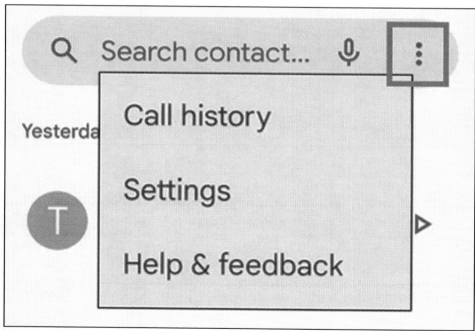

Figure 3.26

When you get to your settings, look for a section called *Sound & vibration* and then look for *Phone ringtone* and then tap on it to get to your ringtone options.

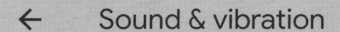

Figure 3.27

Once you are in the ringtones area, you should have several sound categories to choose from. Many of the sounds will be various rings while others will be musical in nature.

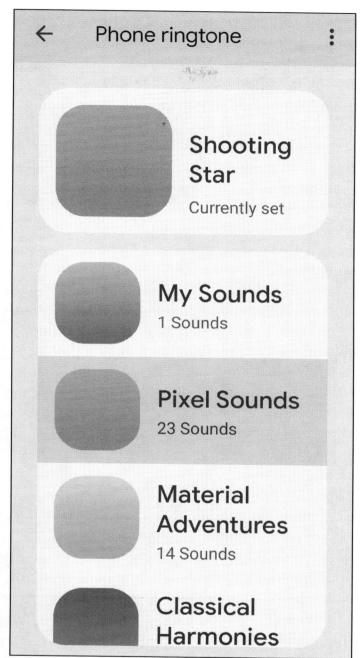

Figure 3.28

When you choose the category you like, you should be able to listen to the ringtone sample by tapping on it. Once you select the one you like, simply tap on *Save* and it will then be your new ringtone. If you change your mind and don't want to use any of the other ringtones, you can just exit the settings, and nothing will be changed.

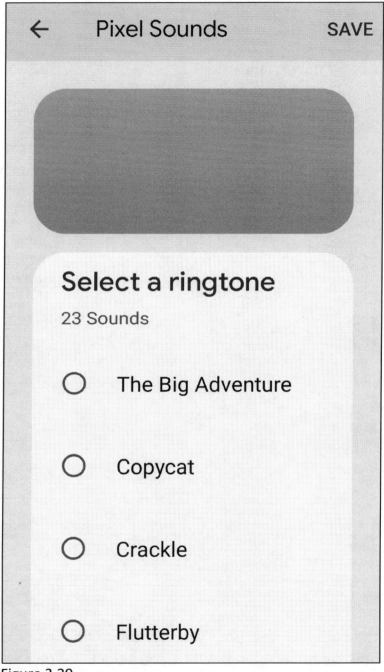

Figure 3.29

Google Assistant

Most people know about Apple's Siri and how iPhone users can say "Hey Siri" to have their smartphone take voice commands for them. Android phones have a similar feature called the Google Assistant. This assistant can also take voice commands such as having it call or text someone from your contact list, set a timer, turn on your phone's flashlight or even tell you a joke.

To access the Google Assistant, simply say "Ok Google" or "Hey Google" to your phone and it should bring up the assistant from the bottom of your screen as seen in figure 3.30.

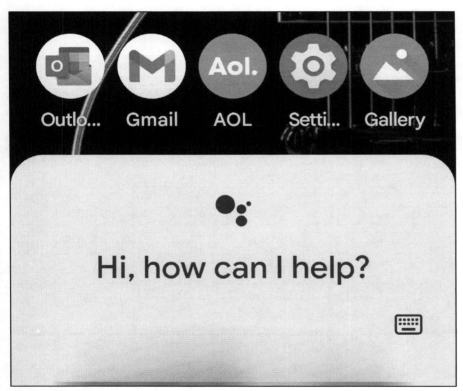

Figure 3.30

Then you can ask it to do something or ask it a question, and if it's capable of fulfilling your request, it will do so. I asked my phone to check the current weather and the results are shown in figure 3.31.

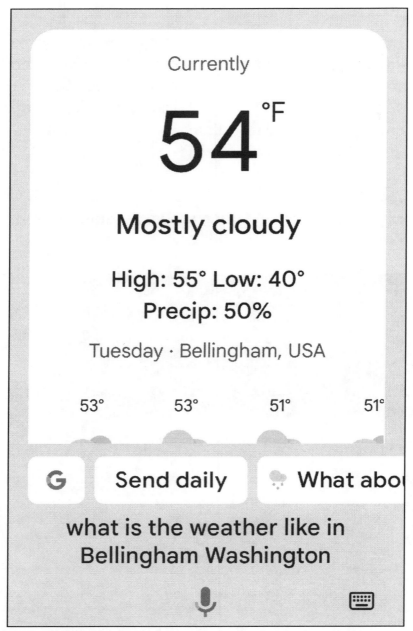

Figure 3.31

The Google Assistant should be enabled by default but if it doesn't seem to be working, you might have to go into your phone's settings to turn it on.

Rebooting vs. Shutting Down Your Phone

I had mentioned how today's smartphones are more powerful than computers from not too long ago and just like computers, you can turn them off and restart them as needed.

As you might have noticed with your computer, it tends to slow down the longer it's been running and after you open and close apps, it can start to run low on resources to keep things running at their best. You might have also had problems on your computer such as it freezing up or crashing and that can also happen with your smartphone.

 If you would like to learn more about how to get the most out of your personal computer, then check out my books titled **Computers for Seniors Made Easy** and **Windows 11 for Seniors Made Easy**.
https://www.amazon.com/dp/B099BYDL4S
https://www.amazon.com/dp/B09XLTCCJK

The button that you use to turn the screen on and off can also be used to shut down or reboot your phone. For most Android models you can hold down on this button to get the power selection screen as seen in figure 3.32.

You should have an option to power off (shutdown) your phone or reboot your phone. If you power off your phone and want to turn it back on, you will need to hold the same button once again until you see something on the screen and then you can let go of it.

For some phones, you might have to do something like press the power button and volume up button at the same time to get the power options but most of the time you can change this configuration so you only need to use the one power button.

Figure 3.32

Restarting your phone should only take a couple of minutes and it's a good way to have your phone "refreshed" and running at its best once again.

Chapter 4 – Installing New Apps

One of the major differences between your old cellphone and your new smartphone is the ability to install apps to add functionality to your phone. You can think of apps as being similar to software that you would install on your computer, such as Microsoft Word or a game for example.

There are thousands of apps available to download and install for just about any task that you can think of. Some examples would be games, word processors, email clients, banking apps, music players, step counters, shopping, navigation and many, many more.

Using the Google Play Store
In order to search for and install apps on your phone, you will need to use the Google Play Store app that comes included on all Android smartphones. The icon will be a blue, green, red and yellow tilted triangle.

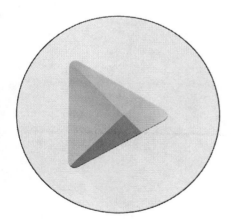

Once you open the Play Store app, you will be shown various categories that you can use to browse the available apps, books and movies. You can even sort by new releases, free apps, top rated, categories and so on.

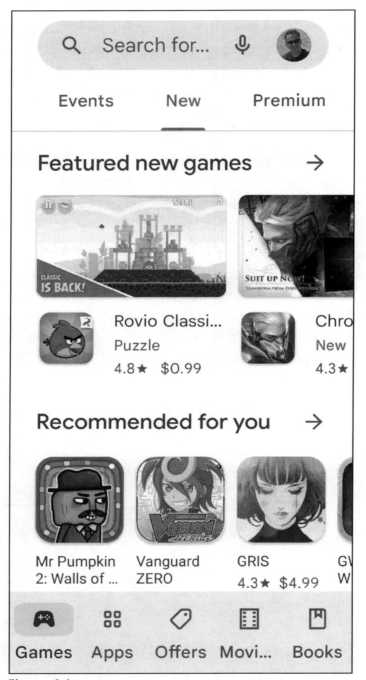

Figure 4.1

To search for a specific app or type of app, you can type your search word or term in the search box at the top of the screen. For my example, I will be looking for the popular *Scrabble* game. Figure 4.2 shows some of the results that I am shown related to my search term.

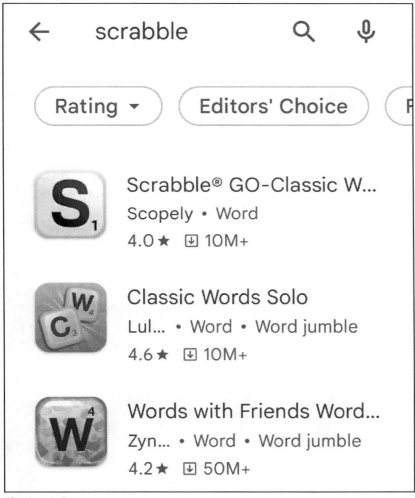

Figure 4.2

I can then tap on one that looks interesting, and I will have a green *Install* button that I can tap on to install the game.

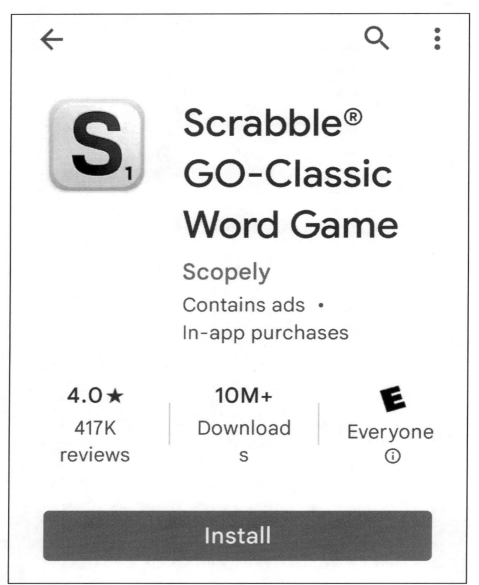

Figure 4.3

What you should always do before installing an app is scroll down on the page and check out things such as the description of what the app does and some of them even have videos or pictures showing how the app looks or works.

About this game →

The Original Word Game with More Ways to Play with Friends!

(#8 top grossing in word)

Figure 4.4

I would also check out the average rating for the app based on all the reviews. You can also read some of the reviews as well while you are there.

When it comes to reviews, I tend to read the 3-4 star reviews since the 5 star reviews might be fake to build up the overall rating of the app and the 1 star reviews can often be people who just like to complain and bad mouth things. I feel the middle of the road reviews are the most accurate.

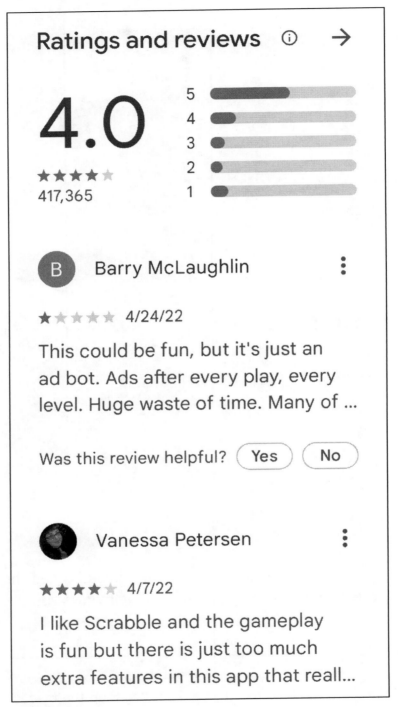

Figure 4.5

If you like what you see and want to install the app, then tap on the Install button to begin the process. Installing an app is very easy and once you tap on Install, your phone should do the rest. Then you will see the Install button change to say *Open* for regular apps or *Play* for games.

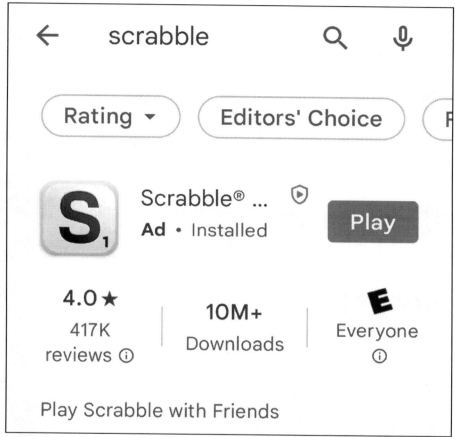

Figure 4.6

You will also find your new app on your home screen if there was room to place an icon for it there. If not, then it might be listed on one of your other screens or you can find it in the area that shows all of your apps.

Like I mentioned before, not all of your apps will be shown on your home screen or other screens but how you find them will vary depending on your phone. Most of the time you can swipe up from the bottom or side to show a listing of all your apps in alphabetical order and then open them from there (figure 4.7). So if you are missing an app, check this section out first before assuming it somehow got removed.

Figure 4.7

Free vs. Paid Apps

When "shopping" for apps on the Google Play Store, you will most likely notice that some of them have a price listed next to them as you can see in figure 4.8. This is because the creators (developers) of these apps put a lot of work into them and want to get paid by selling them to you.

Figure 4.8

As for the free apps, the developers usually make their money by showing advertisements within the app that will randomly pop up while you are using it. So if you don't mind seeing ads while using your apps, you can stick with the free ones but if you find something you really like and there is no free version or you would like to use it without the ads, then you can purchase the app.

When you tap on an app that is not free, you will see the price shown where the Install button would normally be.

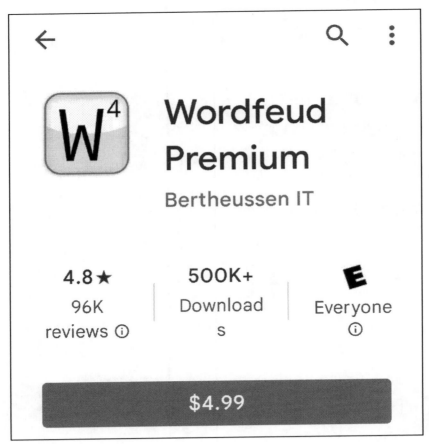

Figure 4.9

If you tap on the price, you will be shown any stored payment options you might have set up that can be used to purchase the app.

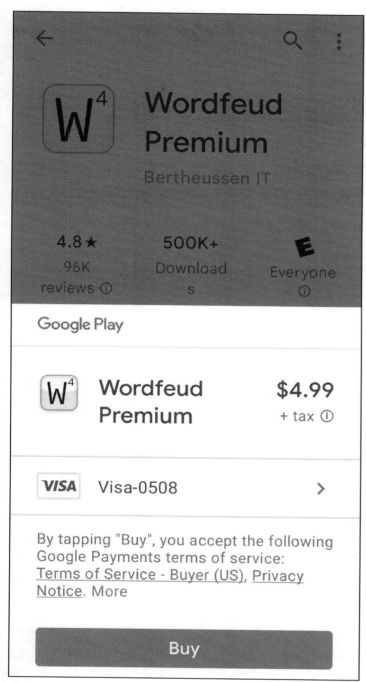

Figure 4.10

If you don't have a payment method in place, you can set one up that can be used for any other apps you might want to buy.

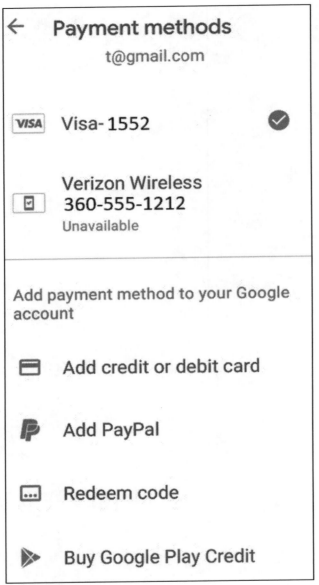

Figure 4.11

In all my years of using Android phone, I have only bought one app and can usually find a free version of whatever I need. If you search hard enough, you can usually find a decent app even if you have to deal with advertisements. You may also have to try out several apps before you find what you are looking for.

Checking App Reviews

Earlier in this chapter, I mentioned how you should look at app reviews before deciding if you want to install the app or not. In this section I will be going a little deeper into how to view these reviews.

When you are looking at the details of a particular app, you will see the reviews section showing the average rating and also a diagram of how many of the reviews are 1, 2, 3, 4 or 5 stars (figure 4.12). You will also see the total number of reviews below the average.

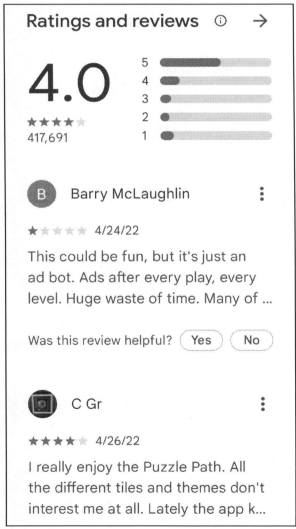

Figure 4.12

Tapping on the 1 through 5-star review diagram will bring you to a different page where you can scroll through the reviews and even filter them by positive, critical, and the number of stars given to the app.

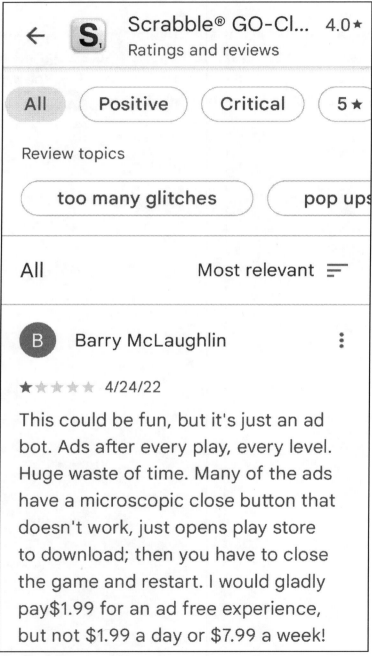

Figure 4.13

Tapping on the three bars next to *Most relevant* will allow you to sort the reviews by most relevant or most recent as well as being able to show the reviews for the latest version of the app only or reviews that apply to your particular phone model.

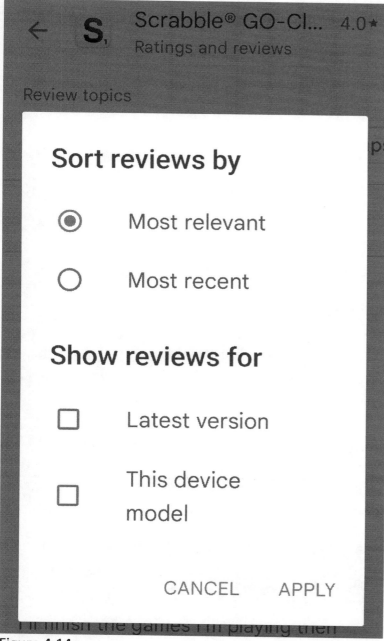

Figure 4.14

You will also be able to give the app your own rating as well as add any comments about the app you wish to share as seen in figure 4.15.

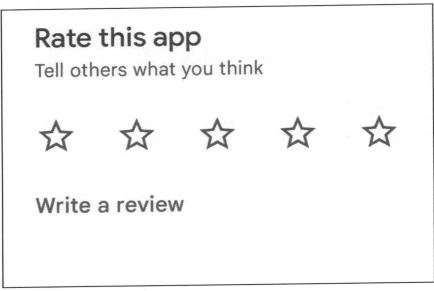

Figure 4.15

Viewing and Closing Open Apps

As you open apps on your phone, they will tend to stay open even if you do not see them on your screen. For the most part, leaving an app open doesn't really affect anything and they are designed to keep quiet in the background until you want to access them again.

After a while, you might find that you have more apps open than you need or want to close an app that you are finished with. If you want to see which apps you have open, you can use the square button at the bottom of your screen if you have the bottom buttons showing.

Figure 4.16

If you don't have the square to tap on, you will need to swipe up from the bottom, but this can be a little tricky because you will need to swipe up from the very bottom, otherwise you will just be taken to your main app listing.

Once you get to the screen where you see your open apps (figure 4.17), you can scroll through them to go back to a particular app or swipe up on an app to close it.

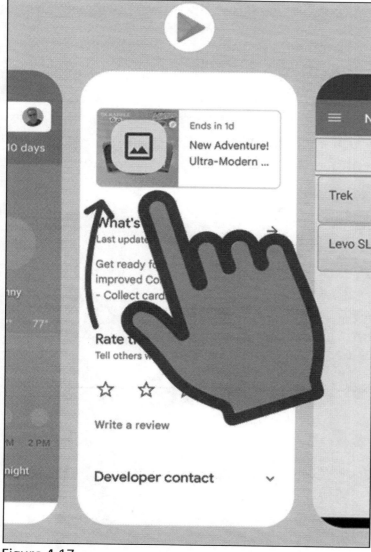

Figure 4.17

You can sometimes close an app from the app itself because some apps will have an exit or close option when you use your back button or swipe left enough times to go back through the app to where you started from.

Uninstalling Apps

As you start installing more apps, you will find that a particular app is not what you are looking for or you don't have a need for an app and want to remove it from your phone to clean things up or make room for other apps.

The process for uninstalling apps is fairly simple and you can do it a few different ways. One way I like to use is to tap and hold the icon for the app and drag it to the top of the screen. You should then have an *Uninstall* option that you can drag the app on to in order to have it uninstalled from your phone (figure 4.18). The *Remove* option will only remove the icon for the app from your screen.

Figure 4.18

You can also long hold on an app icon to bring up the *App info* option that you can then tap on to take you to the information page for the app (figure 4.20).

Figure 4.19

Figure 4.20

Once you are here, you can tap on *Uninstall* to remove the app from your phone.

You can also go to your phone's settings and search for apps and then tap on *See all apps* and find the app you want to remove. Once you find your app and tap on it, you will see the same screen you saw in figure 4.20.

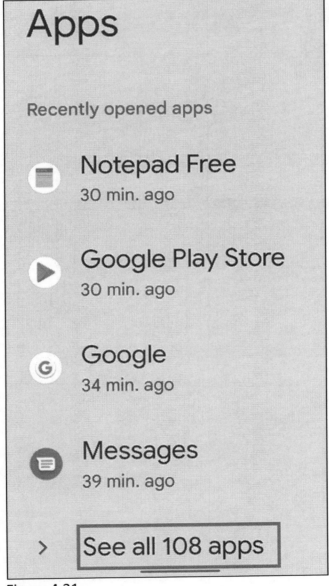

Figure 4.21

Chapter 5 – Texting

One of the most common things that people use their smartphones for is to send and receive text messages, also known as SMS messages. In fact, many people prefer to send text messages rather than actually talking to someone on the phone.

The main benefit of texting is that you can send someone a message and they can read it and reply to you when they have time. Not everyone can answer their phone at any time during the day and if you leave them a voicemail, it's not something they can reply to without having to call you back.

Texting is similar to emailing another person because you can have a back and forth conversation that can go on for as long as you like. Plus you can even add certain types of attachments such as pictures to your messages.

Composing a Text Message
To send a text message, you will need to tap on your text messaging app icon to open your text application.

When the app opens, you will see a listing of any text conversations you have already started. You can then tap on any one of them to continue the conversation. If you want to start a new message with someone who is not on this list, you can tap on *Start chat* (figure 5.1).

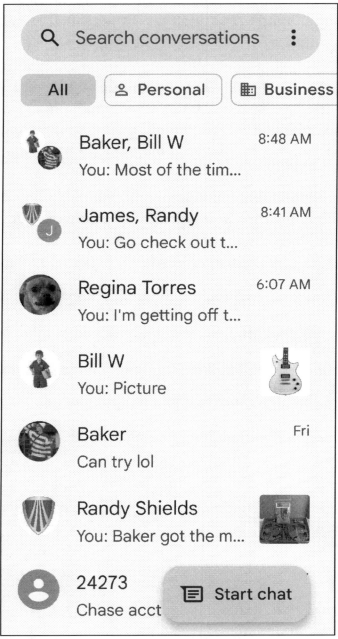

Figure 5.1

You will then be brought to a screen where you can type in the phone number that you want to text. You can also type in the name of the person you want to text and if they are in your contacts, you will start getting suggestions as you type their name (figure 5.3).

The *Create group* option can be used to enter the names or numbers of multiple people so you can start a group text message conversation that anyone in the group can read or reply to.

← New conversation

To   Type a name, phone nu... ⠿

👥⁺ Create group

Top contacts

M&D

...

\# Warranty Center
(866) 406-5154   Home

\#DATA - Data Used
\#3282   Home

Figure 5.2

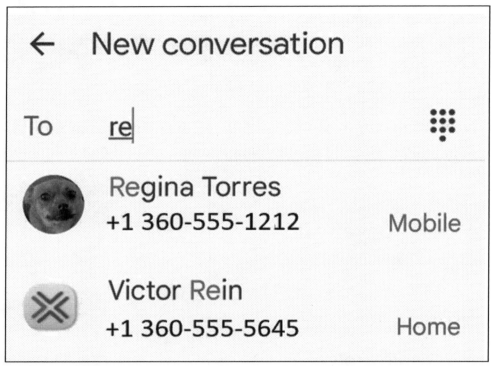

Figure 5.3

Once you enter the number or name, you can then tap in the Text box to type in your message (figure 5.4).

You can also tap on the microphone option to then be able to speak your message into your phone and have it translated as text in case you are a slow typist or have trouble using the keyboard. You can even use punctuation by saying *period* or *question mark* at the end of the sentence to have that character inserted into your message.

If you have another microphone in the box where you actually type the text, that is usually used to record your voice and then send your voice recording via a text message. Then the person on the other end can listen to your recording. This can be seen next to the smiley face in figure 5.4.

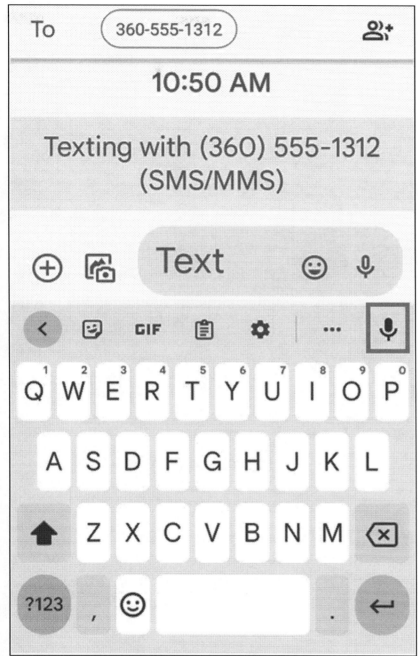

Figure 5.4

Once you have your message composed, you can then tap on the send button which usually looks like a paper airplane.

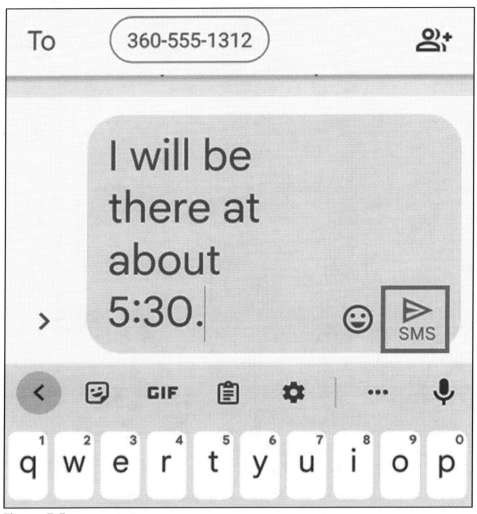

Figure 5.5

You will then see your message and it should say *Now* or *Sent* underneath showing that it was successfully sent to the other person.

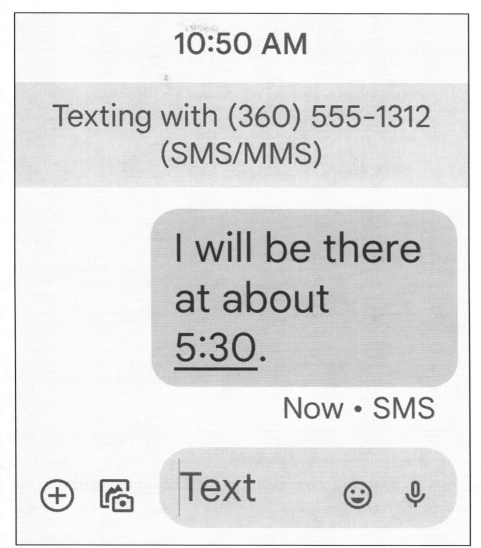

Figure 5.6

Depending on the text messaging app the person on the other end is using, you might be shown when a text message was actually read and also be able to see when they are typing a message back to you (figure 5.7).

Figure 5.7

If you ever want to delete a text message, you can do so by long holding on the message from your main message list to select it and the tap on the trash can icon to delete it. If you want to delete a particular message from a conversation, you can long hold on it to highlight it and then tap the trash can icon as well.

Adding Emoji's

When sending text messages, sometimes it's hard to convey how you are feeling with just words. Or sometimes you might be typing something sarcastic, and you are not sure if the person on the other end will realize that you are joking. This is where using emojis can really help you out.

The word emoji applies to various types of characters such as smiley faces, thumbs up, animals, hearts and many other types of symbols.

You can place one or more of these characters at any place within your text message to convey a particular emotion.

If you look back at figure 5.7, you will see the smiley face icon next to the word Chat. If you were to tap on it, you would see various emojis that are most likely grouped into categories as seen in figures 5.8 and 5.9.

Figure 5.8

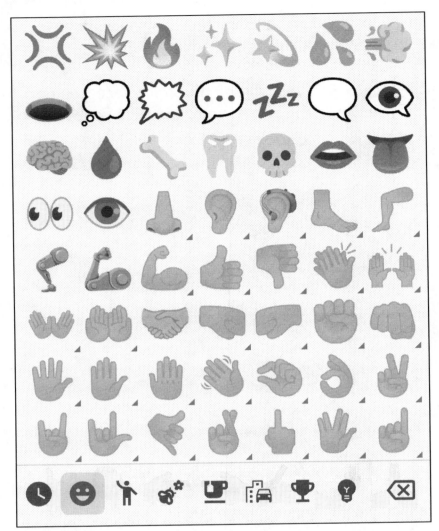

Figure 5.9

To insert an emoji, make sure your cursor is at the right position within your text and then tap on the emoji you wish to use. You can also add more than one in various places if needed.

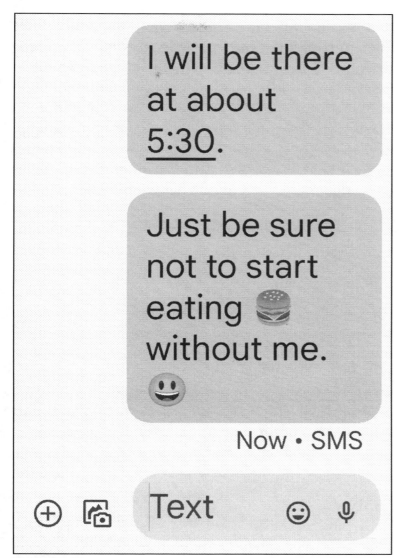

Figure 5.10

Picture and Video Attachments

One of the more popular things that people like to do when it comes to texting, is add photos and sometimes even videos to their text messages. This is a great way to instantly show someone something such as a nice location you are at or even something you have a question about where describing it in words would not do the trick.

You can share photos and videos right from your photo app which I will be discussing later in the book, but most people like to attach a photo or video right from the messaging app itself.

 When you share photos and videos via text messages, the app will reduce the size of the photo or video to make it easier and faster to send. So if you need to send a photo that needs to be full size for printing etc., then you are better off emailing it.

For the most part, you really won't be sending videos unless they are really short because they generally come out so fuzzy on the other end that they are hard to watch so I will be focusing more on sending photos.

To send a photo from your messaging app, you will need to find the *attachment* or *attach photo* button. Figure 5.11 shows that you can tap on the photo icon to attach a picture and next to it you will see the **+** add button that will give you additional attachment options.

Figure 5.11

When you tap on the add photo button, you will be able to take a picture right on the spot and then have it inserted into your text message or you can choose from a photo that is already on your phone by scrolling over to the right. Your phone should show you the most recent photos first.

Figure 5.12

You should also have a Gallery button as seen in figure 5.13. When you tap on this, you will be brought to a view where you can see all your photos and then find the one you want to attach (figure 5.14).

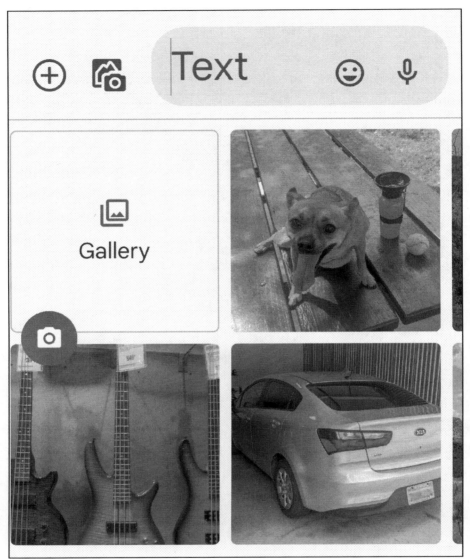

Figure 5.13

Figure 5.14

Once you choose a photo, it will show in the message box with an X next to it that you can tap on if you want to remove the photo before sending the message.

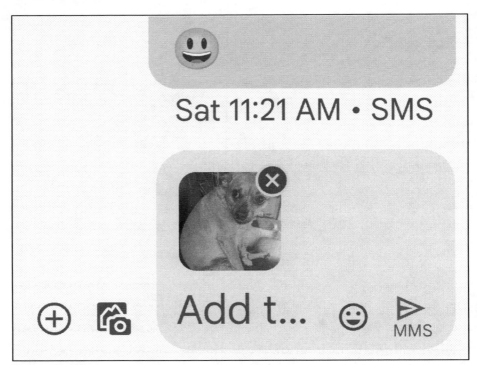

Figure 5.15

Once you tap on the Send button, your will see your picture in the message box and it should say sending and then eventually change to say sent.

Figure 5.16

You can also add text to go along with the picture you send in the same message by simply typing in your message before tapping on the send button. If you want to send more than one picture at a time, you can also do that by selecting multiple photos when choosing the picture you want to send. I would limit this to maybe 3 at a time because you might have trouble sending too many if you overdo it.

Other Attachments

Photos and videos are not the only things you can send in a text message. Depending on your phone model, you will have some other options when it comes to text message attachments.

If you tap on the + button next to the picture attachment button, you should see the other types of attachments you can add to your messages as shown in figures 5.17 and 5.18.

Figure 5.17

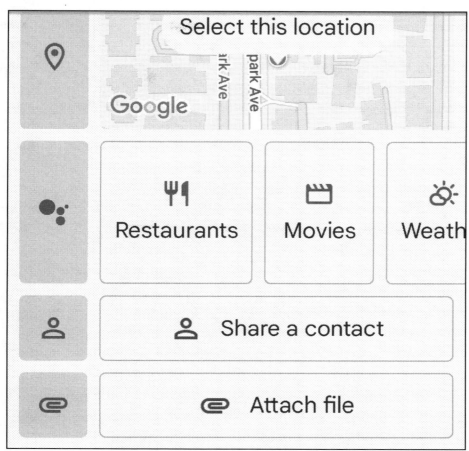

Figure 5.18

Adding an animated GIF is always a fun thing you can do if you want to try and make someone laugh or express how you are feeling at the moment. When you tap on GIF search, you can type in a word or phrase, and it will show you animated images you can attach to your text message. After you chose the one you want, it will be inserted into the message just like you saw for inserting photos.

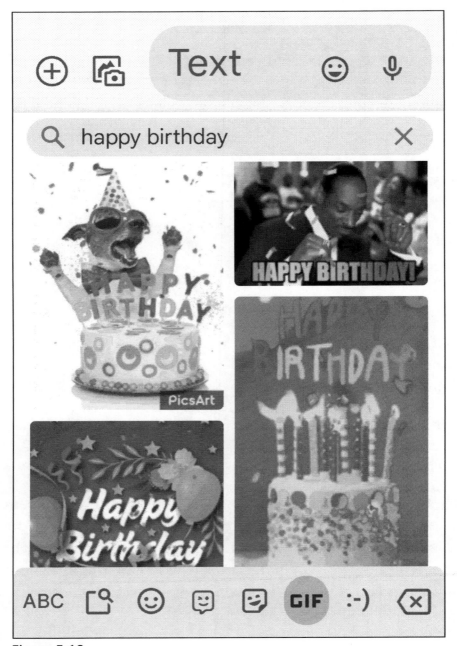

Figure 5.19

The section in figure 5.18 that says restaurants, movies and weather can be used to share local places and weather conditions.

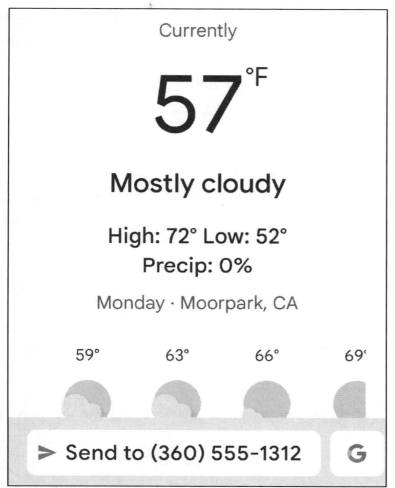

Figure 5.20

The *Share a contact* option is very useful because it will allow you to send the information from one of your contacts to another person without having to type in things such as the phone number etc. manually.

The *Attach a file* option can be used to attach other types of files besides photos such as documents etc. Just keep in mind that the person on the other end might not be able to open your attachment depending on whether or not they have an app to do so.

Select this location can be used to share your current location with another person. This way you can send them a map link that they can open and see your exact location and then they can use that to get directions to where you happen to be. I will be going into more detail about how to use the Maps app in chapter 8.

Forwarding and Sharing Text Messages
Smartphones make it easy to share just about everything including photos, emails, websites, your location and so on, so it makes sense that you can also share your text messages.

Many times, someone will send you a message or a photo and you would like to share that with another person so they can then receive the information or photo. To do so, you can long hold on the message or photo to highlight it and then tap on the three vertical dots at the top right of the screen.

So if I tap and hold on the last message in my conversation as seen in figure 5.21, it will be highlighted, and I can then tap on the three dots and choose to either share or forward the message.

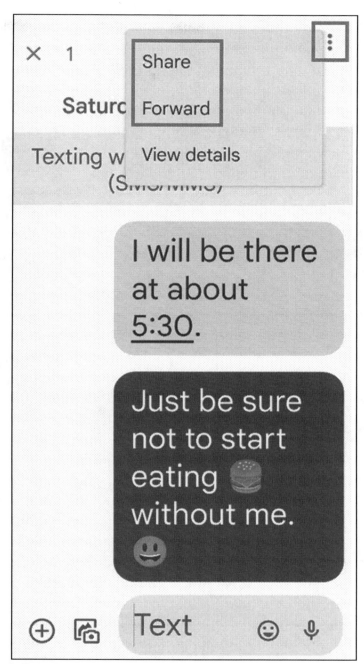

Figure 5.21

If I choose *Share*, I will be able to share the message via text, email or any other app I have on my phone that supports message sharing (figure 5.22).

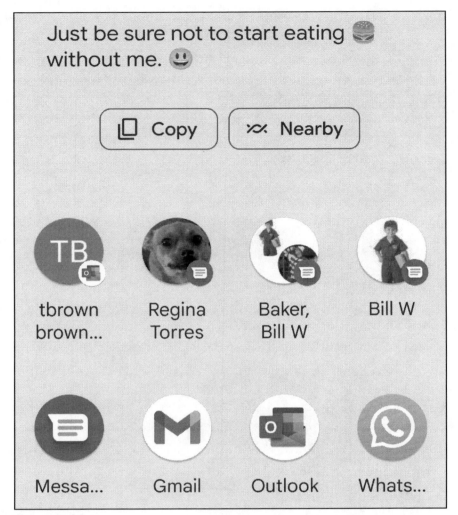

Figure 5.22

For example, if I choose to share with Gmail, it will put the information from the text into a new Gmail email that I can then send out to others.

If you are interested in learning how to get the most out of Google's Gmail email application, then check out my book titled **Gmail Made Easy**.
https://www.amazon.com/dp/B09PW3TRMX

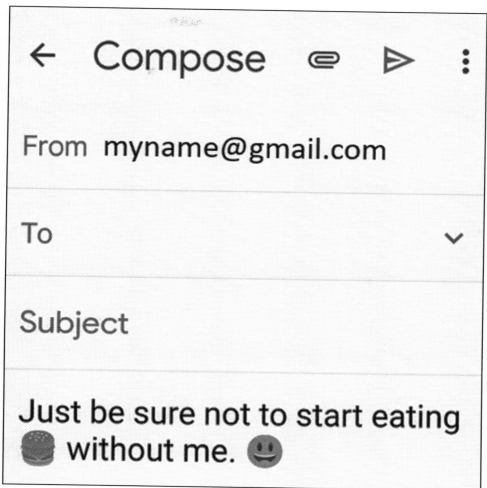

Figure 5.23

If I choose *Forward*, I will only be able to forward it to another text message recipient and I won't have all the other options as I do for Sharing. I can share it in an existing conversation or share it with a new conversation.

Reporting and Blocking Spam Texts
By now, we are all used to spam phone calls and emails and unfortunately there is a growing problem of scammers trying to trick us into buying things or giving out our personal information by sending us spam text messages.

Many smartphones will have an anti-spam feature that can help detect bogus text messages and even phone calls and alert you that the message you have received might be a scam. When your phone detects an incoming spam message, it should pop up on your screen telling you so and then it will put that message in your *Spam & blocked* section that you can then access by tapping on the three vertical dots on your main text message screen.

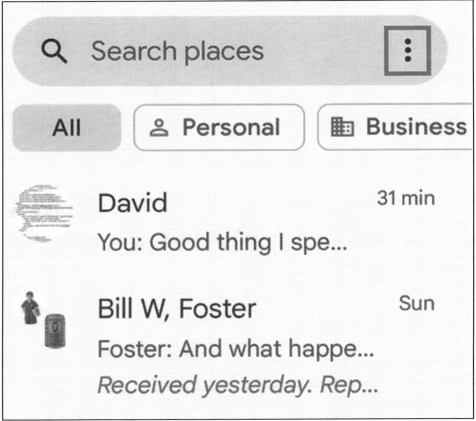

Figure 5.24

Once you are in your spam section, you can view the messages that have been placed there and also delete them if you are sure they are not something you wish to keep (figure 5.25). You can also open them and then choose the *unblock* option to have that number be marked as ok so you will then receive messages from it once again.

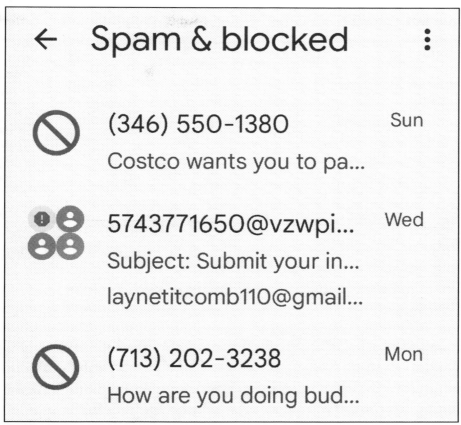

Figure 5.25

To block a number that was not detected as spam, simply highlight the message on your main messaging screen, tap the three dots again and choose *Block*.

On a side note, you can also use this method to add a number you have received a text message from to your contacts by using the *Add contact* option. This works the same way as I showed you for adding phone numbers.

Chapter 6 – Searching the Internet

These days, the internet is so commonly used that if it all of the sudden went away, most people wouldn't know what to do with themselves! The internet is a great place to find information on just about anything and also a place to shop, watch movies, pay your bills and keep in touch with others via social media.

 If you are interested in learning how to use to the most common social media platforms such as Facebook, Twitter and Instagram, then check out my book titled **Social Media for Seniors Made Easy**.
https://www.amazon.com/dp/B09KN64W7M

If you use a personal computer at home, then you have most likely gone online for one reason or another. Since our smartphones are connected to the internet 24 hours a day, it's very easy to open a web browser and search for whatever you might be looking for.

Smartphones have a cellular data connection, meaning that you don't need to be at home or at a coffee shop on a Wi-Fi connection to get on the internet. As long as you have reception on your phone, you can go online from anywhere.

Google Chrome Browser App
In order to get on the internet on your phone, you will need to use a web browser, just like you do on your home computer. If your computer is running Microsoft Windows, you might use the Microsoft Edge browser and if you use a Mac, then you might be using the Safari browser.

Since the Android operating system is owned by Google, your phone should come with the Google Chrome web browser preinstalled. You do not need to use Chrome for your web browser if you have another one that you would like to install from the Play Store.

To open the Chrome browser app, just look for the green, red, blue and yellow Chrome icon on your phone.

Once you have the Chrome app opened, you will see an interface similar to figure 6.1.

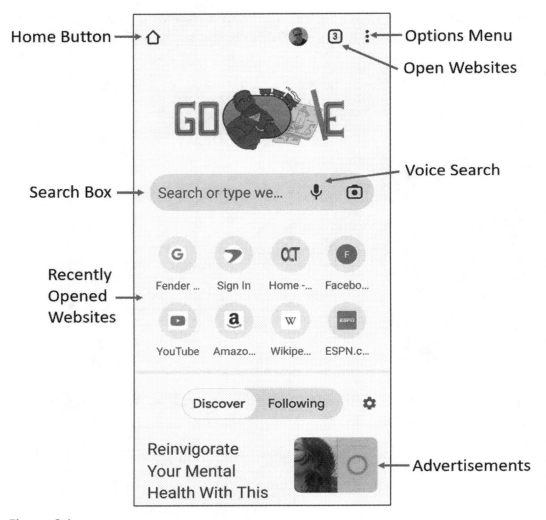

Figure 6.1

Here is a summary of the main sections of the Chrome web browser app.

- **Home button** – This will take you back to the website that you have configured as your main website. By default, Chrome will use google.com.

- **Search box** – Here you can type in search words or terms to then be taken to search results that you can then open.

- **Recently opened websites** – Chrome will list recently accessed websites which makes it easy to go back to those sites once you close and reopen Chrome.

- **Options menu** – There are various settings you can configure within Chrome to make it work more to your liking. I will be discussing some of these in the next section.

- **Open websites** – You can have more than one website or page open at a time. You can use this icon to toggle between your open sites as shown in figure 6.2. All you need to do is tap on the one you want to view. You can also tap on the X at the top right of the preview to close that tab.

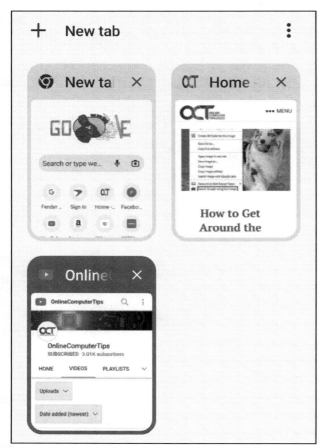

Figure 6.2

Once you are in this area, you can tap on *+ New tab* to open a new tab that will open to your home page where you can start a new search or go to another website without closing the other sites you have open.

- **Voice search** – Tapping on the microphone will let you speak into your phone to tell it what to search for just like you can do with composing text messages.

- **Advertisements** – Just like with everything else, you can't go anywhere without seeing advertisements for stuff you don't need!

Chrome Options Menu
For the most part, you will probably never need to change any of the Chrome options but if you feel like getting adventurous, here is what you can do from here. To open the options menu, tap on the three vertical dots at the upper right corner of the screen.

You will then see a menu similar to figure 6.3. It will have some icons on the top and then some menu options under that.

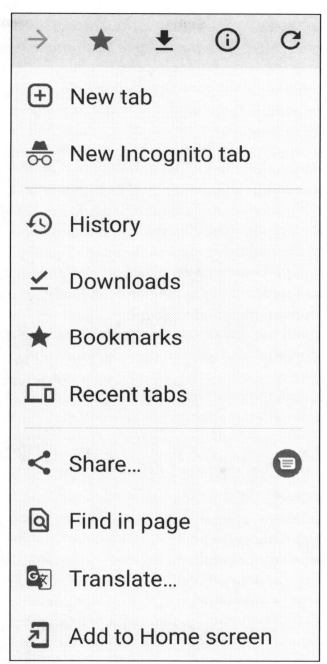

Figure 6.3

Here is what each of these items will do.

- **Right arrow icon** – This can be used to go forward a page on a website if you have first gone back to a previous page.

- **Star icon** – If you want to save a webpage as a bookmark, simply tap on this star icon to do so. Then you will be able to find it listed in the Bookmarks section.

- **Down arrow icon** – This can be used to download the current page you are on so you can view it offline as needed.

- **Circle with an i icon** – If you would like to see information about the page you are on such as the last time you visited it and if it's a secure website or not, you can find that information here.

- **Curved circle icon** – Some websites have information that changes on a regular basis. This icon is called the refresh button and is used to reload the page to its current or updated state.

- **New tab** – As you saw earlier in this chapter, you can have multiple tabs open with a different website in each one. This is another way to open a new tab.

- **New Incognito tab** – If you would like to browse the internet anonymously without your phone keeping track of your history or saving website cookies, you can use this feature to do so.

- **History** – This will show a listing of all the websites you have previously been to. You can also use this to go back to a website you have visited in the past.

- **Downloads** – If you have downloaded any files from a website, this is where you can go to find them.

- **Bookmarks** – Here is where you will find websites that you have saved as bookmarks. I will be discussing this in more detail later in the chapter.

- **Recent tabs** – This is similar to your website history but will show you tabs that you have recently had open. You can then go back to them if you like.

- **Share** – Here you can share websites with other people. I will be discussing this in more detail later in the chapter.

- **Find in page** – This will let you search for a word or phrase on the specific webpage you are on.

- **Translate** – If you go to a site that is not in English (or whichever language you are using), you can have Chrome translate it for you so you will be able to read it.

- **Add to Home screen** – This will place an icon to the website you are visiting on your home screen for easy access.

Performing Website Searches

If you use a computer at home to go online to browse the internet, then doing so on your phone should be very easy to get the hang of since it works the same way.

If you use the same search engine at home and on your phone, it will be even easier. By search engine, I mean Google, Bing, Yahoo etc. which are websites used for searching the internet. And there are web browsers such as Chrome, Edge, Firefox etc. which are the software or apps that you use to open these search engines on. Hopefully that is not too confusing!

If you haven't changed any settings for your Chrome app, then Google should be your search engine by default which is fine for most users. Once you open Chrome, you will have your search box where you can type (or speak) your search term or phrase into the box and Chrome will actually give you some suggestions as you type as seen in figure 6.5.

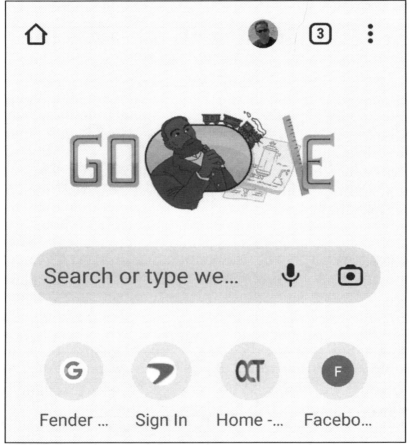

Figure 6.4

If you want to use one of the suggested search terms, you can simply tap on it to have it applied to your search. If you want to search for exactly what you typed in the search box, you can then tap on the search magnifying glass icon to perform the search.

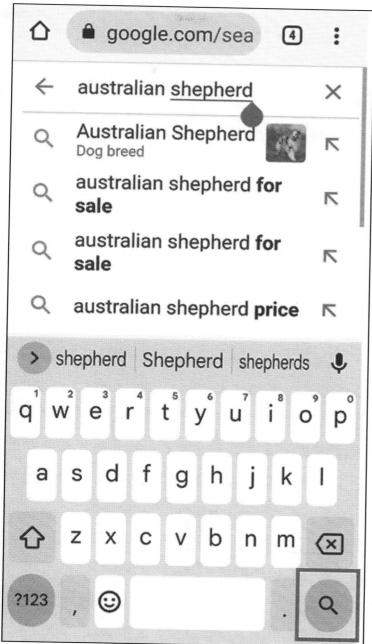

Figure 6.5

You will then be shown the results of your search and from here you can tap on any result that looks interesting to you.

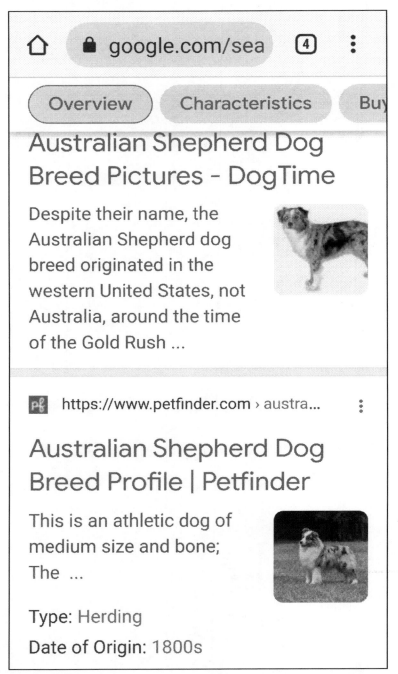

Figure 6.6

Once you start going through your search results, you can use the back and forward buttons to navigate your way around. If you want to go back to your main search page, you can tap on the Home button next to the search box.

Figure 6.7

Bookmarks

If you are a regular internet user, you most likely have some websites that you frequently like to visit and might find yourself searching for the website each time you want to go back to it. Bookmarks were created to make it easier to go back to these websites that you like to visit on a regular basis. You might have also heard the term favorites which means the exact same thing.

Bookmarks are very easy to create and then access once you create them. You can have multiple bookmarks, but you don't want to have so many that it takes you more time to find your bookmark than it would to just do a search for that website. Bookmarks are also useful to mark a specific page on a website that you might not be able to find too easily doing a website search.

To create a bookmark, go to the page you want to create it for and then from the options menu I previously discussed, you can tap on the star icon and you should see a message at the bottom of your screen saying the page was bookmarked.

Now when you go to that page and tap on the options menu, your bookmarks star should be filled in solid showing this page is in your bookmarks.

Figure 6.8

To access your bookmark, you can go to the options menu and then to bookmarks. You might have a section called *Mobile bookmarks* that will have the bookmarks you created on your phone (figure 6.9). Here you will find your bookmarks and can simply tap on the one you want to open to be taken right to that page.

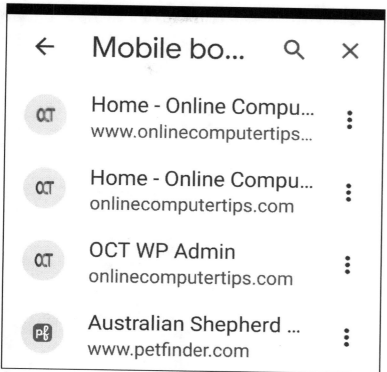

Figure 6.9

If you were to tap on the three vertical dots next to a bookmark, you will have options to do things such as edit, delete and move it up the list.

Sharing Websites with Others
Since everyone is into sharing everything, they do with each other these days, it only makes sense that we can share any website that we happen to be on with other people.

There are multiple ways of sharing when it comes to our smartphones and the methods you have will vary depending on what apps you have installed on your phone. For the most part, you can share most things via text message and email very easily.

If you are on a website and want to share it with another person, you can tap on the three vertical dots once again and then tap on the *Share* option.

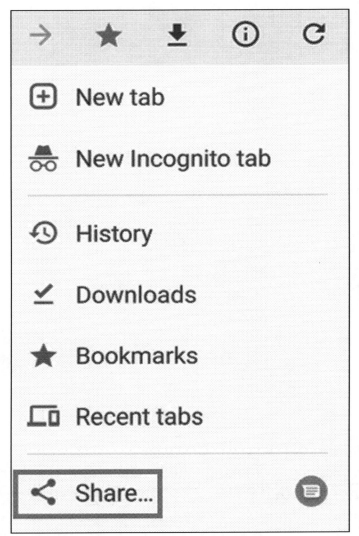

Figure 6.10

You will then be presented with the more commonly used apps on your phone that you can choose from to share the website. You will also notice at the bottom of figure 6.11, that you can do things such as take a screenshot (picture) of the webpage or copy the website address and then paste either one of these into an email or other app and send it off to someone else.

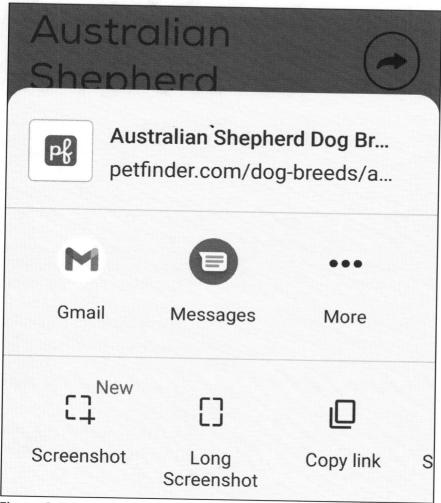

Figure 6.11

If you tap on *More*, you will be shown additional apps that you can use to share the website.

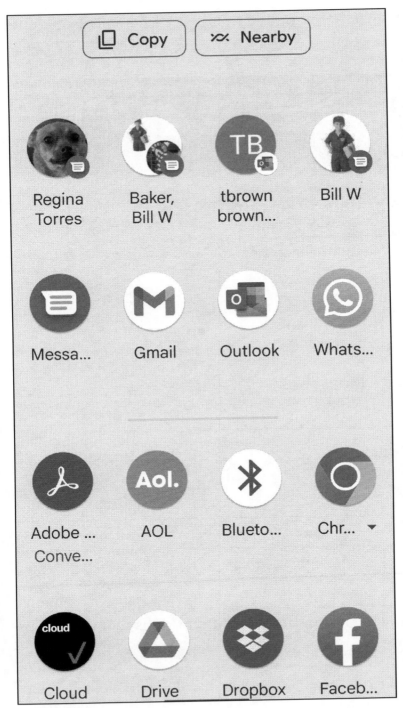

Figure 6.12

I will choose the Messaging option to share the website via a text message. I will then be prompted to choose an existing conversation that I have in my text message area, or I can start a new message.

After I choose the message, I want to share the webpage with, it will automatically be added to the compose box of my text message. I can then send it as is or add a comment above or below the website link.

Just be sure not to add anything to the link text itself, otherwise it won't work when they try and open it.

Figure 6.13

When I send the message, it will be shown in the text conversation and may or may not include a thumbnail image and description of the website I am sharing as seen in figure 6.14. This information is taken from the website itself so that will decide if there is anything like this to show.

Figure 6.14

Now when the person on the other end taps on this message, they will be taken to the same webpage using whatever web browser app they have installed on their phone.

Chapter 7 – Using the Camera

One of the best parts about owning a smartphone is being able to take high quality photos any time and any place, assuming you always carry your phone with you. Today's smartphone cameras take better photos than the dedicated digital cameras we used to use only a few years ago. The quality of your camera will greatly depend on which smartphone model you have so keep that in mind. You would expect a $1000 smartphone to come with a top of the line camera!

Another benefit of having a camera is that we can take a picture and instantly send it to someone else, so they don't have to wait to see whatever amazing thing you are taking a picture of. Plus smartphones come with high resolution video cameras allowing us to take high quality movies any time we find something we think needs to be recorded.

Front vs. Rear Cameras
Most smartphones will come with two cameras built into them. One will be located at the back of the phone and the other will be located at the front. The reason for this is if you need to do something like a video call where you need to see your screen and have your face recorded at the same time, you will need a camera located on the front of your phone. And of course for those who love to take selfies, a front camera is a must so you can see how you look before taking the picture!

The rear camera will be a better quality camera that supports higher resolution pictures and will have more megapixels. This is because most pictures and videos will be taken with the rear camera and selfies and video calls do not necessarily need to be super high quality.

Figure 7.1 shows the placement of the rear and front cameras, and you can see the difference in size and how the rear camera has multiple lenses to increase the quality of the photos. Not all smartphones will have such high end cameras, usually just the more expensive ones.

Rear Camera   Front Camera

Figure 7.1

Taking Pictures & Camera Settings

The process of taking pictures is fairly straightforward but there are a few things you should know to make the experience as trouble free as possible. Your camera will also have a variety of settings to help make your pictures come out as professional looking as they can. To open your camera simply tap on the camera icon. Many times you can press the screen on\off button two times fast to have it open the camera app for you.

The first thing to keep in mind is that there are two ways to take pictures and videos and they are portrait and landscape. The mode you use will determine what gets captured in your photo or video. As you can see from figure 7.2, portrait mode will allow you to capture taller shots while landscape works better for wider shots. Your phone will automatically rotate the screen when you turn the phone a certain way. If you ever find that it's not doing this, check to see if your auto-rotate setting got disabled.

Figure 7.2

At the bottom of your screen when you are using the camera app you will have various buttons depending on your phone model. Figure 7.3 shows that this phone has three zoom presets labeled .6, 1x (default) and 2 times magnification. Of course you can always use your fingers to "pinch" zoom in and out until you find the right zoom level. The big button in the middle is what you will tap on to take the picture and your last picture will be shown to the right in the preview circle. You can tap on the preview to view your last photo. The double arrow icon to the left is used to swap between the rear and front camera.

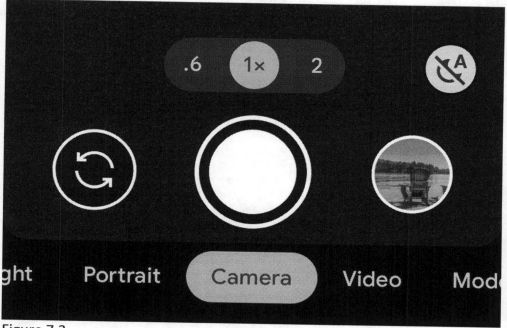

Figure 7.3

Figure 7.4 shows how these buttons look when you use the camera in landscape mode.

Figure 7.4

To switch to video mode, you should be able to tap on the word Video at the bottom of the screen. After that, things will look a little different and once again, your options will vary depending on your phone.

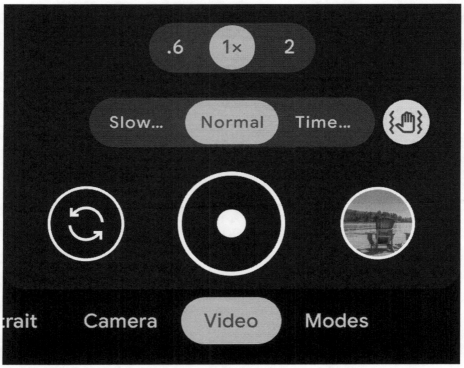

Figure 7.5

When you tap on the record button in video mode, it will most likely turn red and then start a timer showing you how long you have been recording. You will also have a pause button and you can the record button should change to a stop button that you can tap on to stop the recording.

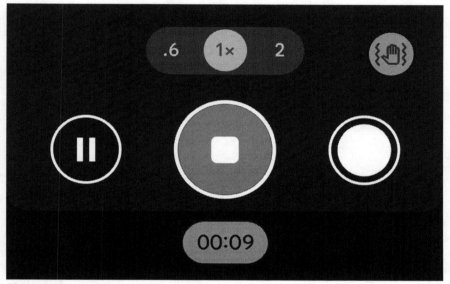

Figure 7.6

 Videos take up much more space than photos so be aware of that when recording your videos. It's easy to run out of storage space on your phone when you record a lot of videos. The same can even apply to photos is you are the type who likes to take pictures of everything!

Viewing and Organizing your Pictures and Videos

After you take a bunch of photos, you are most likely going to want to view them as well as show them to others. There are many photo viewer apps that you can download and install to view your pictures, but your phone should come with a built in app called **Google Photos**.

This app will let you view your pictures and videos and also do things such as delete and share them and even edit them if needed.

To open the Photos app, look for the red, blue, yellow and green icon that looks similar to the image below. You have probably noticed that Google uses these colors on almost all their app icons.

Once you open the Photos app, you will see your photos and videos organized by date. You will be able to tell which are photos and which are videos because the videos will have a play button on them as well as the length of the video (figure 7.7). All you need to do to view one is tap on the preview image to open it full screen as seen in figure 7.8.

Figure 7.7

Figure 7.8

Once you have the photo open you will have various options as to what you can do with it.

Top icons

- **Back arrow** – This will take you back to the previous screen.

- **Upload button** – Android devices will automatically backup your photos and videos to "the cloud," meaning your online Google Photos account so if you ever lose your phone or get a new one, they should sync up and all be there after you configure your new phone. The *upload* button will do a manual upload to your online photo storage just in case the automatic method did not work.

- **Star icon** – This will add a particular photo to your favorites, making it easier to find later. More on favorites in a minute.

- **Three vertical dots** – If you need to see details about a photo or video such as when it was taken or where it was taken, you can find this here. You can also add a photo to an album, delete it, order prints and other options from this section.

Bottom icons

- **Share** – Just like with everything else, you can share photos and videos as well. I will be discussing this in more detail in the next section.

- **Edit** – Google Photos will let you edit your photos in regard to brightness, contrast, tint, color and so on. You can also do things such as crop your photo or add a custom filter to it to give it a custom look.

Figure 7.9

- **Lens** – Google Lens will analyze your photo and try and find similar matches to your photo online. This can come in handy if you are out somewhere and see something you like and would then like to find it online to maybe buy one for yourself.

- **Delete** – If you don't want a photo or video any longer, you can delete it from here.

 If you end up using a different photo viewer app, keep in mind that Google will still backup your photos and videos online. So if you delete a photo from your new app, there will most likely still be a copy of it in your online account that you will have to delete from there as well.

The *Library* section of the Photos app will show you the various categories that Photos uses to store your pictures and videos. You will have your main Camera section that shows pictures you took just using your camera the normal way.

There will also be sections for *Messages* that contain pictures you took using the text messaging app. You might also have sections for screenshots, downloads and so on depending on whether or not you have used the camera for these purposes.

Figure 7.10

At the top of the Library section you will have categories such as *Favorites* and *Trash*. Any photo that you added by tapping the star icon will be shown here. If you have deleted a photo or video and want to restore it, you can do so by going to the trash section.

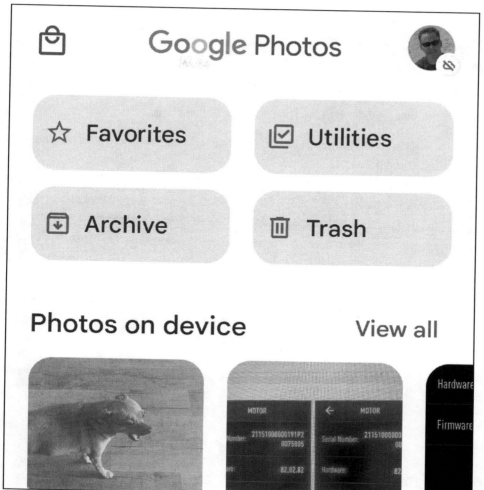

Figure 7.11

Photos will let you create albums that you can then move pictures and videos into in order to help keep them organized. You can also do this on the Photos website if you prefer working on your computer rather than your smartphone. Any changes you make via your computer will be reflected on your phone and vice versa. To access your pictures and videos online, you will need to go to the Photos website and log in with your Google account. Then you will see a similar looking interface and all your pictures and videos as seen in figure 7.12.

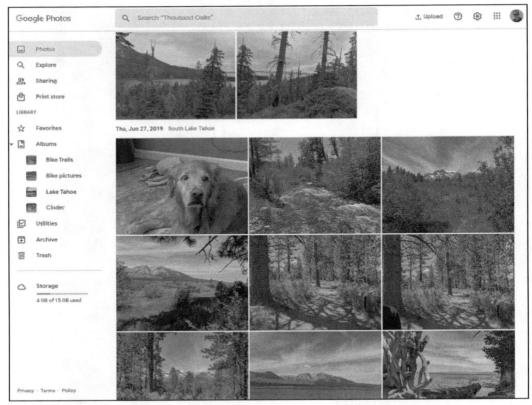

Figure 7.12

Sharing Your Photos

One of the best reasons to take pictures is so you can share them with friends and family, whether they want to see them or not! There are several ways to share your pictures as you saw when I attached a picture to a text message. You can also attach them to emails and share them with social media apps such as Instagram and Facebook.

If you are using the Photos app to view your pictures, you can open the photo you want to share and then tap on the *Share* icon to start the process. If you are not using the Photos app then you should still have a share option within whichever app you are using.

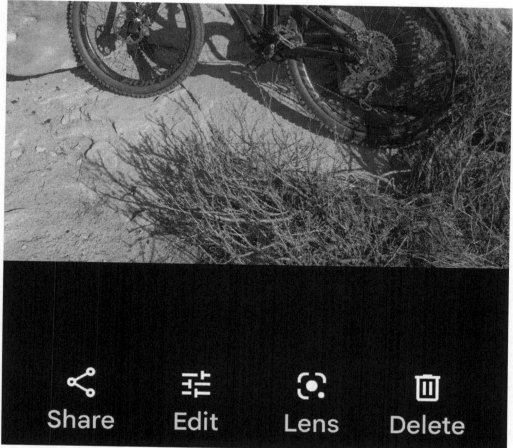

Figure 7.13

You will then see the familiar sharing options which will vary depending on what apps you have installed on your phone.

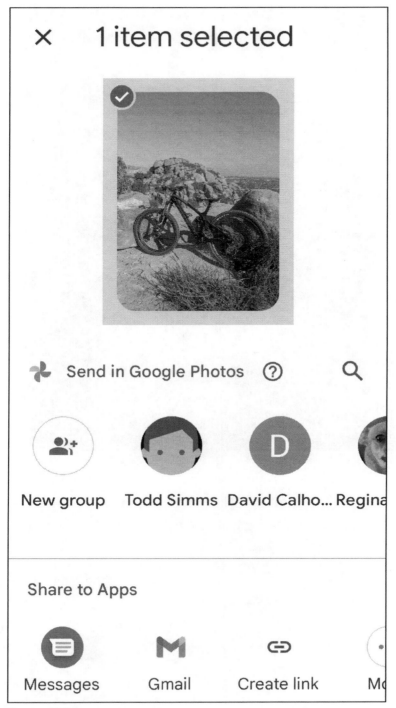

Figure 7.14

Tapping on *More* at the bottom right will bring up additional choices as seen in figure 7.15. Many of these choices you will most likely never use.

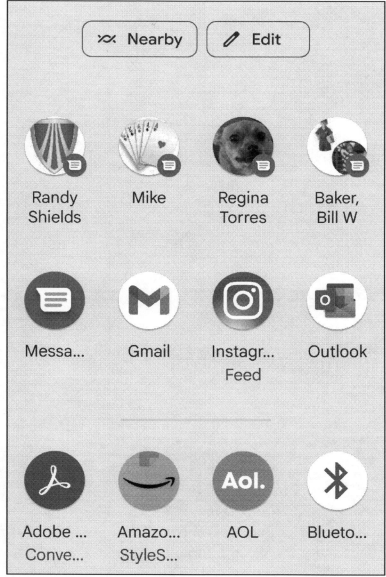

Figure 7.15

I will choose Gmail as the app I want to share my photo with, and my phone will automatically add the picture as an attachment to a new email. I can then fill out the recipient information, subject line and a message to go with the photo.

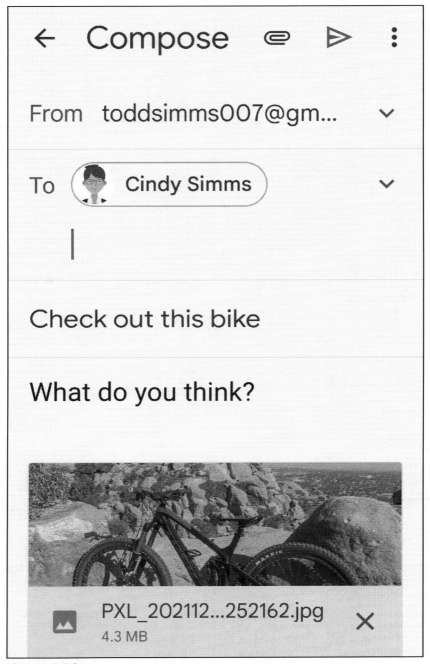

Figure 7.16

Checking Your Phone's Free Space

If you plan on taking a lot of photos, and especially if you will be taking a lot of videos, you might find yourself running out of room on your phone before you know it. Everything that is on your phone takes up storage space, including the apps themselves and any documents or other files you might have saved on it.

If you are curious to see how close you are to running out of space, you can go to your Settings app (gear icon) and then look for a section called *Storage*.

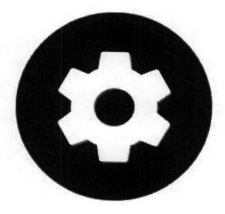

You might be shown the percentage of your storage that has been used without even tapping on the Storage section itself.

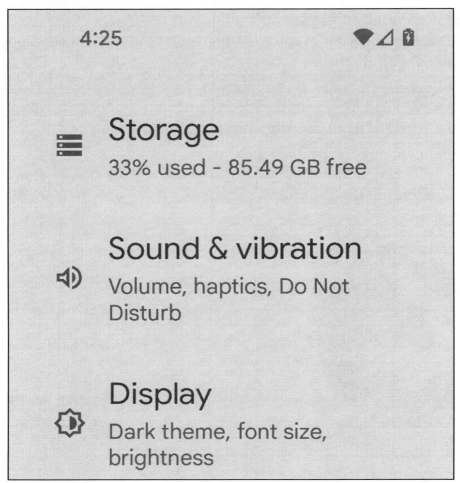

Figure 7.17

Once you access the storage section, you will be shown more details as to what items are using your phone's storage space. Figure 7.18 shows that my images are using 685 MB (megabytes) out of my total storage space of 128 GB (gigabytes). If you feel like doing some math, there is 1024 MB in 1 GB.

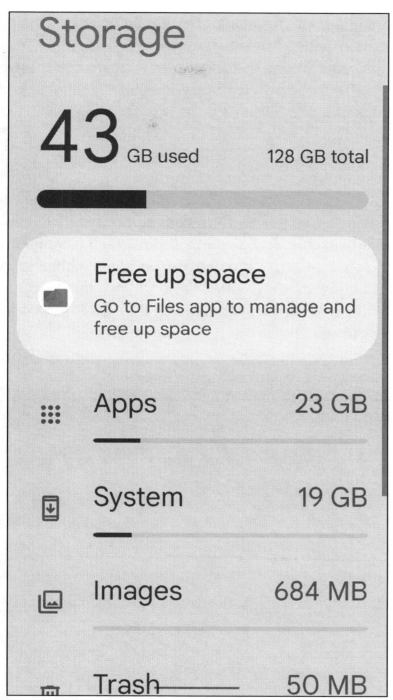

Storage

43 GB used   128 GB total

Free up space
Go to Files app to manage and free up space

Apps   23 GB

System   19 GB

Images   684 MB

Trash   50 MB

Figure 7.18

Once you start running out of storage space, you will not be able to take any more photos or videos or even install any more apps. You might even notice that your phone will start to slow down and maybe even freeze up on you. To free up space, you will need to either delete some photos or videos or uninstall some apps you don't use.

Transferring Pictures and Videos to Your Computer
One way to get the storage space back on your phone without deleting your photos or videos is to transfer them to your computer. There are two ways you can go about this. You can copy them over which means you will have the same photos and videos on your phone and computer. Or you can move them to your computer and remove them from your phone which is what you will need to do if your goal is to free up space on your phone.

The first step in the process is to connect the USB cable that came with your phone to the normal charging port on your phone, and then to a free USB port on your computer.

Figure 7.19

The next step involves telling your phone that you want to use the connection to your computer to transfer files. This is usually done by pulling down from the notification area, tapping on the USB section (figure 7.20) to open up the connection options, and choosing the appropriate action (figure 7.21).

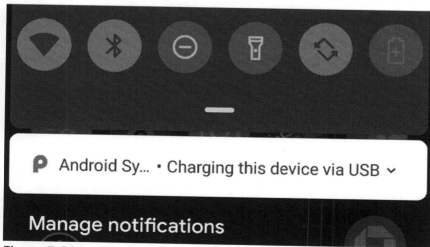

Figure 7.20

Notice in figure 7.21 that I chose the *File Transfer* option because I want to transfer files from my phone to my computer. You may see options with slightly different names such as *photo transfer,* for example.

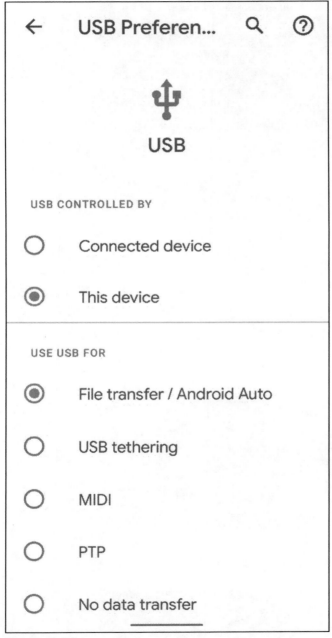

Figure 7.21

Then on my computer (I'm running Windows), I should see my phone appear. Then I can double click on its internal storage to see the files and folders contained on my phone.

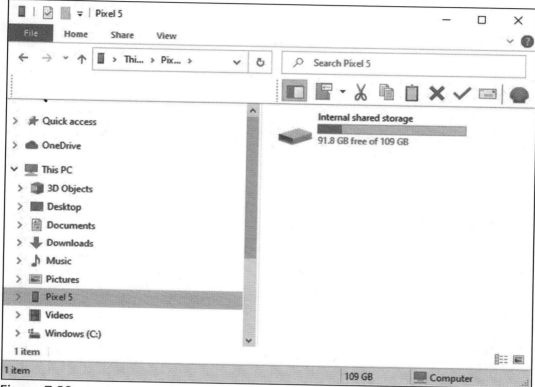

Figure 7.22

The folder I want to look for is named DCIM, and when I find that, I want to double click it to open it up.

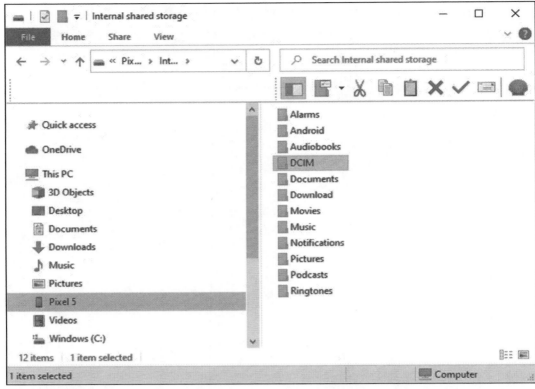

Figure 7.23

Within that folder you may see your pictures, or you might have another folder called *Camera* that you will need to open up. Once you are here, you can drag and drop the pictures from your phone to your computer and then delete them off your phone after you confirm that they have been copied over. You can delete them using the phone, or you can delete them right from this DCIM folder that you opened on your computer.

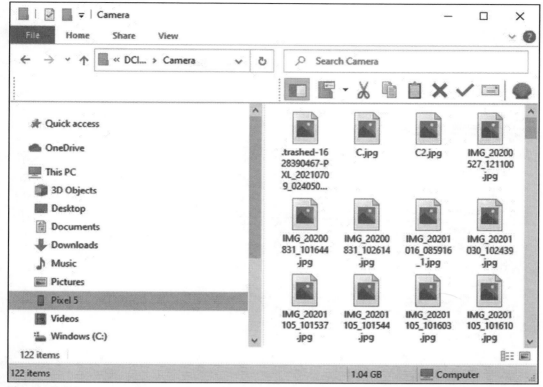

Figure 7.24

If you are looking for pictures that were sent via text message or saved from taking screenshots, then you can look for a folder named *Pictures* rather than DCIM, and inside that folder you should find what you are looking for.

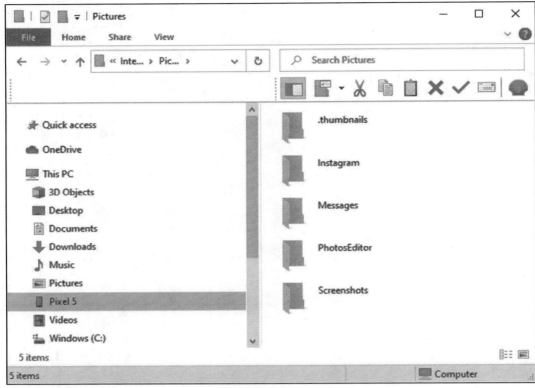

Figure 7.25

Chapter 8 – Google Maps Navigation

If you find yourself driving to places you have never been before, having a navigation system is an invaluable tool to help you get there or to save you when you get lost. Sure many cars come with built in navigation but if yours doesn't or if you simply want to get some directions to just about anywhere when not in your car, your smartphone can certainly help you out.

The Google Maps App
When it comes to smartphone and even PC maps and navigation, Google Maps is the king. Even iPhone users will install the Google Maps app on their phones because it does such a good job. To open Google Maps, look for the "pin" looking icon that will once again be blue, green, yellow and red.

Once the app opens, it should use your phone's internal GPS to find your location and then show you some options you can use to find places in your local area. It will even show some of the local businesses on the map and you can tap on them to get more information such as their address, phone number and hours.

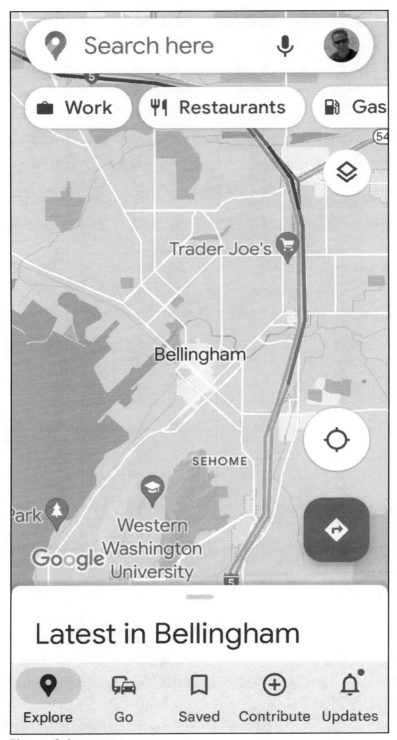

Figure 8.1

You also then use your finger to scroll around the map and then pinch-zoom to zoom in and out of a location. When you zoom in, you will notice that you will be shown more detail in regard to businesses and other places.

Changing Map Views

The default map view used by the app will be the street view. If you tap on the layers icon as seen in figure 8.2, you can choose a different view as seen in figure 8.3.

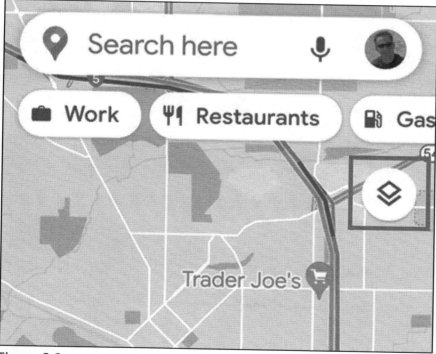

Figure 8.2

You can choose the satellite view to show satellite imagery of the location you are viewing as seen in figure 8.4 or even turn on the traffic layer which will show the traffic conditions in real time on the map. Green indicates no traffic while orange indicates a slowdown and red means its bumper to bumper!

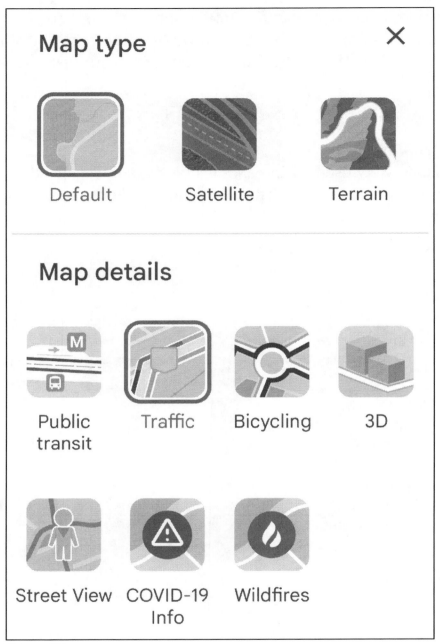

Figure 8.3

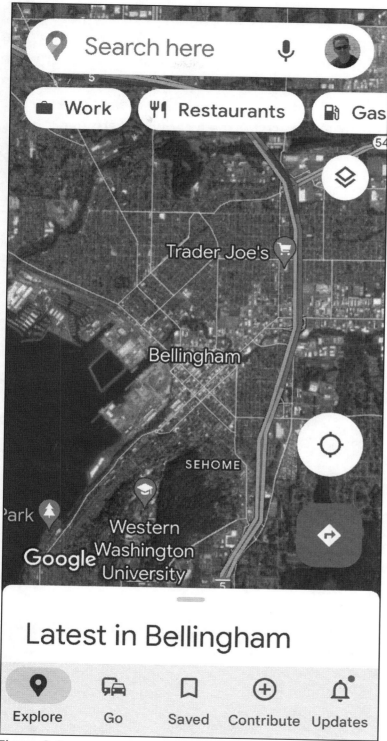

Figure 8.4

There are other views as well, but they are not as useful. One view you may find that comes in handy is the *Street View*. This will give you a street level image of the location you are looking at as if you were actually there. It's supported on most streets but if you find the option unavailable for the location you are looking at, that means that Google never mapped out the area. If you ever see a car with a strange looking device on the roof, it might be Google mapping out the area and taking pictures for the Street View feature.

Figure 8.5

If I were looking at the Luxor Hotel in Las Vegas using the satellite view on my phone, it would look similar to figure 8.6.

Figure 8.6

If I were to turn on the Street View layer, then any street that supports this view would be highlighted in blue and I can tap on that part of the map\street to be taken to the street imagery as seen in figure 8.7.

Street View

I can then use my finger to pan around the image as well as zoom in and zoom out. If I were to tap on one of the arrows on the street, I can then virtually move up and down the street as if I were actually there. This is one of those features that you really need to try for yourself to fully understand how it works, so give it a shot!

Figure 8.7

Searching for Locations

One of the most common reasons for using the Map app is to find the location of a certain location such as a restaurant, park, doctor's office, friend's house and so on.

To find these types of locations, all you need to do is type in what you are looking for just like you would in your web browser. If I want to find *Italian restaurants*, I can type that in the search box and Maps will search the area of the map that you are on (figure 8.8).

It will show the restaurant's name and its location with a pin on the map. The numbers shown indicate the average rating for the restaurant. I can then tap on any of the locations to see more details such as their address and phone number.

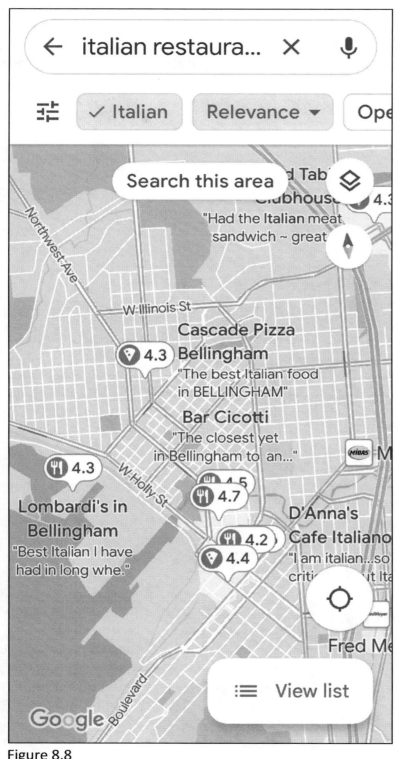

Figure 8.8

I can also tap on the *View list* button to be shown a listing of all the locations the Maps app found for me (figure 9.9). I can then scroll through this list and when I find something that looks interesting, I can then check out any available photos and even a menu for the restaurant.

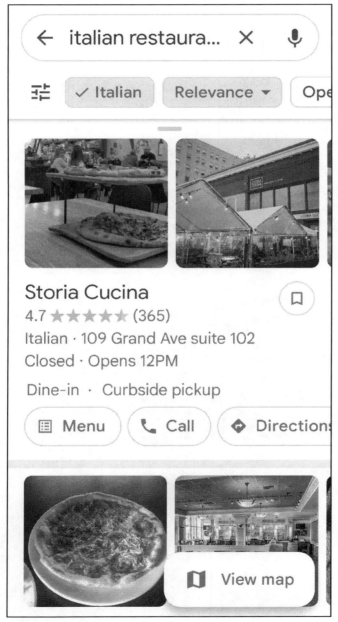

Figure 8.9

Getting Directions (Navigation)

Once you find the place you are looking for, you might need to get directions in case you are not familiar with the street it is on or have never been to that part of town.

If you tap on the *Directions* button while viewing the location, you will need to specify a starting point and will be shown your home address if you have configured it within your Google account as well as previous locations you have looked up. The icons above Home in figure 8.10 are used to tell Maps how you are getting to your destination so it can base your route on your method of transportation. If you are walking for example, you would want to tap on the walking person figure so Maps will not do something like send you on the freeway since that would not be a good thing to do while walking!

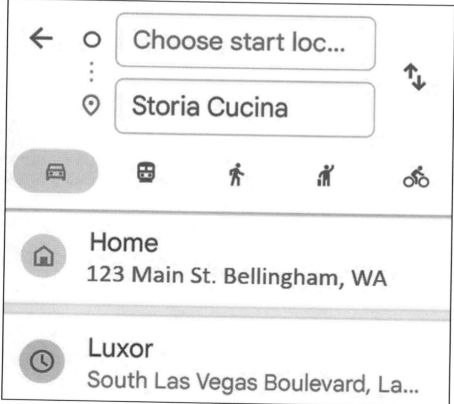

Figure 8.10

If you tap in the *Choose start location* box, you will be able to choose the *Your location* option which will use the GPS within your phone to find exactly where you are so you can start navigating from your current location. Or if you want directions based on a different location then you can choose your start point on the map itself. Most of the time you will want to use the Your location option.

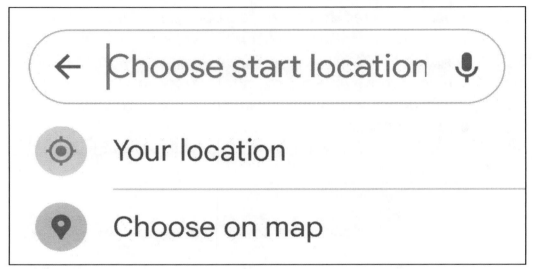

Figure 8.11

Google Maps will then show you the route to your destination highlighted in blue along with the distance and the estimated time it will take to get there. It may show additional routes in grey that you can tap on to make the active route and you can also see any difference in distance or time between routes (figure 8.12).

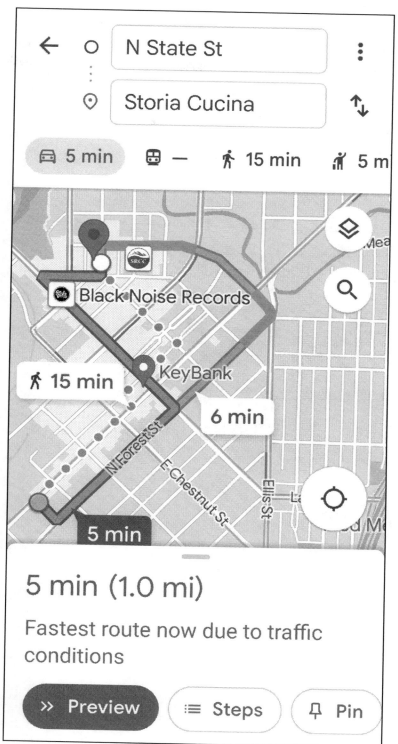

Figure 8.12

If I were to tap on the walking person figure, it would then update my route distance and time to reflect how long it would take to get there via walking.

Figure 8.13

I can even choose the bus option to see information about bus routes and pickup times.

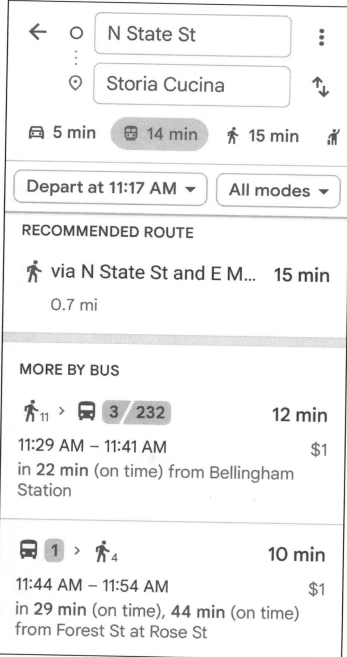

Figure 8.14

If I were to tap on the *Steps* button at the bottom of the screen, I would then be shown step-by-step directions with pictures I can tap on to view in order to get a visual idea of where I will be going (figure 8.15).

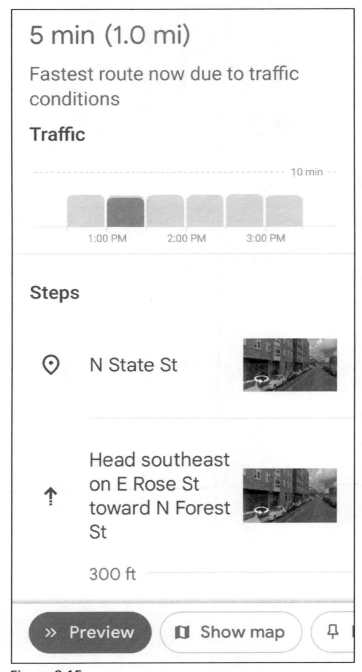

Figure 8.15

Sharing Locations

If you need to share a particular location with someone else so they can meet you there for example, it's very easy to do so right from the Maps app itself.

Once you find the place you wish to share, simply tap on the *Share* button just like you would to share any other type of item from your phone.

Figure 8.16

Then you will be presented with the same items you have seen before and just need to determine how you want to share this location.

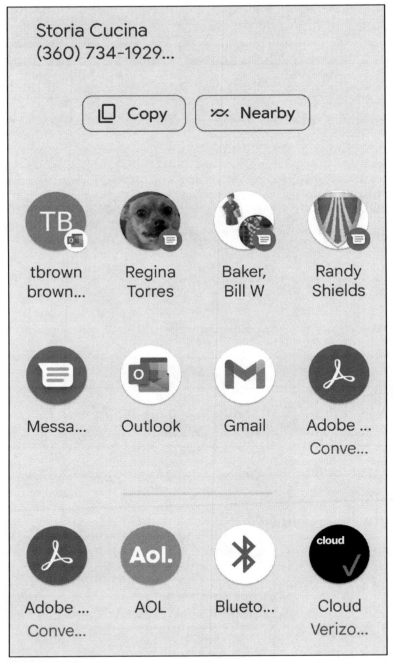

Figure 8.17

I will choose to share the location via my Gmail app and once I tap on the Gmail icon, the information will automatically be entered into the email and all I will need to do is type in the recipient's email address and any extra information I want to include in the email.

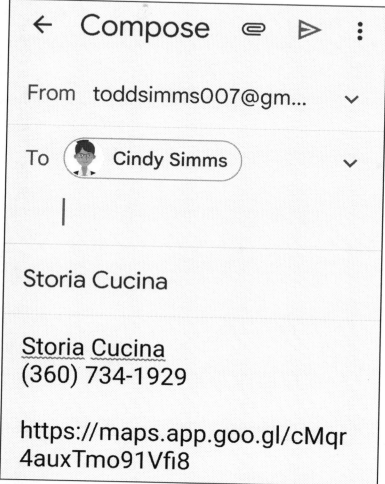

Figure 8.18

Then when they receive the email on their end, it will appear as shown in figure 8.19, and they can simply click on the link either on their phone or computer and be taken to that location in Google Maps.

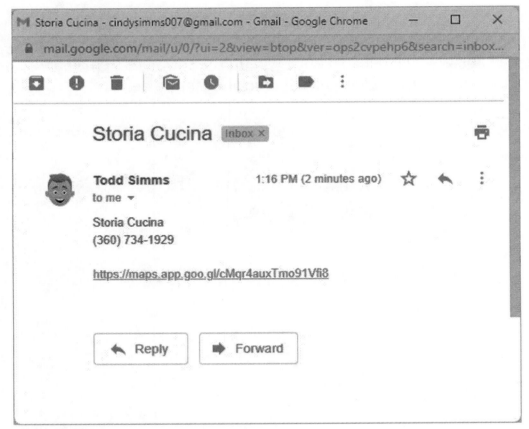

Figure 8.19

What's Next?

Now that you have read through this book and taken your Android smartphone skills to the next level, you might be wondering what you should do next. Well, that depends on where you want to go. Are you happy with what you have learned, or do you want to further your knowledge on Android devices?

If you do want to expand your knowledge, then you can look for some more advanced books or ones that cover the specific technology that interests you such as Android operating specific book. Focus on one subject at a time, then apply what you have learned to the next subject.

There are many great video resources as well, such as Pluralsight or CBT Nuggets, which offer online subscriptions to training videos of every type imaginable. YouTube is also a great source for instructional videos if you know what to search for.

If you are content in being a proficient smartphone user that knows more than your friends, then just keep on practicing what you have learned and don't be afraid to poke around with new apps, settings, and other configurations because you might be surprised at how well you can make your Android phone work for you and have it do things you didn't think were possible.

Thanks for reading **Android Smartphones for Seniors Made Easy.** You can also check out the other books in the Made Easy series for additional computer related information and training. You can get more information on my other books on my Computers Made Easy Book Series website.

https://www.madeeasybookseries.com

You should also check out my computer tips website, as well as follow it on Facebook to find more information on all kinds of computer topics.

www.onlinecomputertips.com

https://www.facebook.com/OnlineComputerTips/

About the Author

James Bernstein has been working with various companies in the IT field for over 20 years, managing technologies such as SAN and NAS storage, VMware, backups, Windows Servers, Active Directory, DNS, DHCP, Networking, Microsoft Office, Exchange, and more.

He has obtained certifications from Microsoft, VMware, CompTIA, ShoreTel, and SNIA, and continues to strive to learn new technologies to further his knowledge on a variety of subjects.

He is also the founder of the website onlinecomputertips.com, which offers its readers valuable information on topics such as Windows, networking, hardware, software, and troubleshooting. Jim writes much of the content himself and adds new content on a regular basis. The site was started in 2005 and is still going strong today

Made in the USA
Las Vegas, NV
20 April 2024

88932398R00105